센치한
Listening

감성 맞춤 내신 공략

길들이기

마무리 **1**

woongjin
compass

센치한 **LISTENING** 길들이기 　마무리 1

출판일	1판 1쇄 발행 2014년 8월 29일

지은이	김민주, William Winchester
펴낸이	최회영
책임편집	김소연, 이수미
영문교열	이윤선, 윤은지, 강소영, Peggy Anderson
디자인	성윤지, 노영남, 이보람
펴낸곳	(주)컴퍼스미디어
출판신고	1980년 3월 29일 제 406-2007-00046 © ㈜ 웅진씽크빅 2011
주소	서울특별시 서초구 서초2동 1360-31 정진빌딩 3층
전화	(02)3471- 0096
홈페이지	http://www.compasspub.com
ISBN	978-89-6697-783-3

이 책의 구성과 특징

01

Introduction

Unit에서 학습의 초점이 되는 주요 의사소통 기능과 예문들을 먼저 학습합니다.

02

Words

듣기평가에서 자주 출제되는 특정 주제의 중요 어휘를 익힙니다.

03

Check Up

01~02. 앞서 배운 의사소통 기능을 중심으로 구성된 짧은 내용을 듣고, 간단한 연습 문제를 풀어봅니다.

03. 빈칸에 알맞은 의사소통 표현을 써 보면서 해당 표현들을 확실히 기억합니다.

04

Actual Test

핵심 의사소통 기능을 포함한 내용으로 구성된 8문항의 문제를 풀어봅니다.
다양한 유형의 실전 듣기평가 문제 유형을 익힐 수 있습니다.

05

Dictation

Actual Test 8문항의 스크립트를 다시 듣고 빈칸을 채우면서 주요 표현과 어휘를 복습합니다.

06

모의고사

실전과 똑같은 스타일로 구성된 총 3회의 모의고사를 통해 실제 듣기평가 시험에 완벽 대비합니다.

Table of Contents

이 책의 구성과 특징   3

UNIT I   I CAN'T STAND IT.   6

UNIT II   DON'T WORRY ABOUT IT.   12

UNIT III   CAN YOU MAKE IT AT 4?   18

UNIT IV   HOW DID YOU LIKE IT?   24

UNIT V   DON'T YOU THINK SO?   30

UNIT VI   CONGRATULATIONS!   36

UNIT VII   WILL YOU DO ME A FAVOR?   42

UNIT VIII   WHY DO YOU THINK SO?   48

UNIT IX   PLEASE LET ME TRY.   54

UNIT X   I HOPE TO VISIT PARIS ONE DAY.   60

UNIT XI   ARE YOU WITH ME?   66

UNIT XII   WHAT DO YOU MEAN?   72

별책 부록

모의고사 1회

모의고사 2회

모의고사 3회

정답 및 해설

A Separate-Volume Supplement : Answers and Audio scripts . MP3 File CD

UNIT I I CAN'T STAND IT.

문제에 대해 묻기

무슨 일이니?	What's wrong? / What's the matter? What's the problem?
무슨 일이 있었니?	What happened?

부정적인 감정 표현하기

～을 참을 수가 없어.	I can't stand ~. / I can't put up with ~.
～이 지겨워지고 있어.	I'm getting tired of ~.

긍정적인 감정 표현하기

그 말을 들으니 기뻐.	I'm glad to hear that.
～라니 기쁜걸.	I'm happy / glad (that) ~.

Words   *Relationships*

- agree with
- chat with
- conflict
- depend on
- friendship
- generation
- have ~ in common
- marriage
- misunderstanding
- put up with
- senior
- social

01 대화를 듣고, 이번 시험 성적에 대한 여자의 생각을 나타낸 그림을 고르세요.

 02 대화를 듣고, 내용과 일치하면 T, 일치하지 않으면 F에 ✓ 표 하세요.

1 The girl is excited about giving a report in class. ⬜T ⬜F
2 The boy feels nervous when he gives a speech or report. ⬜T ⬜F

03 주어진 표현을 사용하여 대화를 완성하세요.

What's wrong	I'm glad that	I'm getting tired of	I'm happy to

A John, you seem to be angry today. _____?
B _____ doing so much work after school.
A I know what you mean. I have a lot of homework, too.
_____ the class will be over soon.
B Yes, _____ know that as well. We can both get some rest!

들려주는 내용을 잘 듣고 물음에 답하세요.

1 대화를 듣고, 여자의 차를 고르세요.

①   ②   ③   ④   ⑤

2 다음을 듣고, 무엇에 관한 내용인지 고르세요.

① 사람의 모습을 한 컴퓨터   ② 컴퓨터끼리 경쟁하는 퀴즈 쇼   ③ 퀴즈 쇼에서 우승한 컴퓨터
④ 퀴즈 문제를 내는 컴퓨터   ⑤ 질문에 대답하는 컴퓨터

3 대화를 듣고, 포스터에 표시된 내용 중 대화에서 언급되지 않은 것을 고르세요.

EARTH DAY FESTIVAL
① Live music, Farmer's Market, Vegan Food,
② Student Art Exhibition, Mini Eco-Film Festival
③ All for FREE!
④ Thursday, November 10, 2011
⑤ Alumni Mall

4 대화를 듣고, 대화가 일어나는 장소로 가장 알맞은 곳을 고르세요.

① train station   ② bus stop   ③ subway station
④ airport   ⑤ taxi stand

5 다음을 듣고, 아래 그래프에서 <u>틀린</u> 부분을 고르세요.

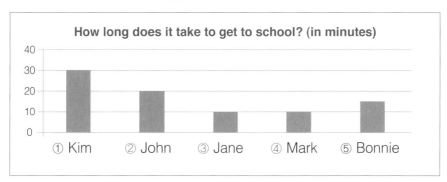

6 대화를 듣고, 친구 Amy에 대한 여자의 의견으로 가장 알맞은 것을 고르세요.

① She is forgiving.   ② She is rude.   ③ She is funny.
④ She is loving.   ⑤ She is annoying.

7 다음을 듣고, 남자가 좋아하는 일을 고르세요.

① 친구들과 어울리는 것   ② 외식을 하는 것
③ 가난한 사람들과 이야기를 하는 것   ④ 어려운 사람들을 돕는 것
⑤ 병원을 방문하는 것

8 대화를 듣고, 왕실 결혼식에 대해 언급되지 <u>않은</u> 것을 고르세요.

① the dresses   ② the church   ③ the hats   ④ the music   ⑤ the princess

다음을 듣고 빈칸에 들어갈 알맞은 말을 쓰세요.

1

M Hi, Jill. _____ _____?

W I _____ _____ where I parked my car. Can you _____ _____ _____ it?

M _____ _____ _____ _____. Can you describe it?

W Well, it is a _____ _____ _____.

M OK. Is it a large car or a small one?

W It is small and has _____ _____ _____.

M Is that it over there?

W Oh, there it is. Thanks.

2

W Are computers _____ _____ people? Some people say yes and _____ _____ _____. But one computer _____ _____. Its name is Watson. In February 2011, Watson appeared on the American _____ _____ *Jeopardy*. He competed against some _____ _____ _____. Surprisingly, Watson answered more questions than any of _____ _____ _____! Now that computers can _____ _____ _____ _____, just imagine what the next generation of computers will do!

3

M Hi, Mary. I think I have a problem.

W _____ _____ _____, Paul?

M I can't go to the Earth Day festival _____ _____.

W Oh, no! But there will be _____ _____, food, and an _____ _____!

M I know. I really want to go. I was especially excited about the films.

W So _____ _____ _____ go?

M I have a conflict. I need to study that day.

W _____ _____ _____ on Wednesday instead.

M Great idea. _____ _____ _____ at Alumni Mall!

W _____ _____ _____ _____!

4

W Good morning, sir. How can I help you?

M Hi. I _____ _____ _____. I need to change my ticket.

W Sure, _____ _____ _____ _____ help. What do you need to change?

M Well, this ticket says I have an _____ _____.

W Would you rather have a _____ _____?

Dictation

M Yes, thank you. I _____ _____ sitting near the aisle.

W I _____ _____ you. I like to look out the window when I fly.

5

W Mrs. Smith asked her students _____ _____ _____ _____ them to get to school. Then she put some of the results in a graph. Kim said she _____ _____ _____ _____ _____, because it takes her _____ minutes. John said it takes him _____ minutes. He _____ _____ _____, but lives nearby. Jane said it _____ _____ _____ _____, because her mother drives her. Mark and Bonnie both _____ _____ _____, so it takes them both _____ minutes to get to school.

6

M _____ _____ _____, Martha?

W My friend Amy and I had a fight.

M Wow. I thought you and Amy had a great friendship.

W We do. I just _____ _____ _____ _____ her attitude sometimes.

M _____ _____ _____ _____?

W Well, I gave her a gift, and she said she didn't like it.

M _____ _____ _____. What did you do?

W I told her _____ _____ _____ _____ other people's feelings.

M Maybe it was a misunderstanding.

7

M Sometimes I like to _____ at the local soup kitchen. _____ _____ _____ _____ where poor or homeless people can get a free meal. I _____ _____ I'm really helping my community. Other times, I like to go to _____ _____. I spend an hour or two chatting with senior citizens. They sometimes get lonely and need someone to talk to. _____ _____ _____ _____ to help them feel better.

8

M Did you watch _____ _____ _____ on TV?

W _____ _____ I saw the wedding. It was the social event of the year!

M It was really beautiful. _____ _____ _____ were so fancy. And the hats!

W I thought some of them _____ _____.

M I guess you're right. But _____ _____ was really amazing.

W Oh yes. It's called Westminster Abbey. It's very old.

M _____ _____ _____ the prince and princess are so happy together.

W _____ _____ they will have a wonderful marriage.

II DON'T WORRY ABOUT IT.

UNIT

후회 표현하기

나는/너는 ~했어야 했어.	I/You should have ~.
나는/너는 ~하지 말았어야 했어.	I/You shouldn't have ~.
~에 대해 미안하게 생각해.	I feel sorry about ~.
~했으면/하지 않았으면 좋았을 텐데.	I wish I'd ~. / I wish I hadn't ~.

긍정적인 감정 표현하기

(그것에 대해) 걱정 마.	Don't worry (about it).
너무 마음 쓰지 마.	Don't take it so hard.
	Don't be so hard on yourself.
기운 내.	Cheer up.

Words *Health*

- breathe
- cure
- flu
- infection
- insurance
- medical
- mental
- mind (n.)
- muscle
- patient (n.)
- sickness
- stress
- suffer from

01 대화를 듣고, 남자가 가고자 하는 병원의 위치를 고르세요.

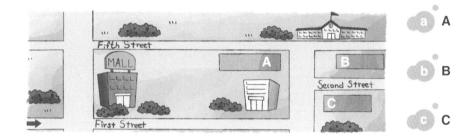

ⓐ A

ⓑ B

ⓒ C

 02 대화를 듣고, 상황을 가장 잘 나타낸 문장을 고르세요.

a A man and woman are shopping for a vase.

b A man and woman are making a deal.

c A woman wants to sell her old vase.

03 주어진 표현을 사용하여 대화를 완성하세요.

you shouldn't have	I wish I had	I feel sorry about	Don't worry

A Dad, I'm the one who broke your computer. _____ not telling you the truth.

B Well, _____ lied to me.

A I know. _____ told you the truth before. But I was afraid you'd be mad.

B _____. I can replace the computer. But I'm glad that you learned a lesson.

들려주는 내용을 잘 듣고 물음에 답하세요.

1 대화를 듣고, 남자의 심정으로 가장 적절한 것을 고르세요.

① peaceful   ② confused   ③ worried
④ confident   ⑤ sad

2 다음을 듣고, 무엇에 관한 내용인지 고르세요.

① 건강한 삶을 사는 법
② 스트레스가 건강에 미치는 영향
③ 스트레스로 인한 질병의 치료약
④ 스트레스의 원인
⑤ 스트레스에 좋은 요가

3 대화를 듣고, 남자의 마지막 말에 대한 여자의 응답으로 가장 적절한 것을 고르세요.

W

① I have to go now.
② Thank you, sir.
③ What is the matter?
④ Call me later.
⑤ Cheer up!

4 대화를 듣고, 두 사람의 관계로 가장 적절한 것을 고르세요.

① 엄마 – 아들   ② 간호사 – 의사   ③ 간호사 – 환자
④ 교사 – 학생   ⑤ 의사 – 환자

5 다음을 듣고, 내용을 통해 추론할 수 있는 것을 고르세요.

① Smith 씨는 건강 상태가 매우 좋다.　　② Brown 씨는 종합 건강 보험에 가입했다.
③ Smith 씨는 보험 자격 요건에 미달된다.　　④ Brown 씨는 보험에 대해 잘 알지 못한다.
⑤ Smith 씨는 회원 자격에 대해 이의를 제기했다.

6 다음 그림에 나타난 상황에 맞는 가장 적절한 대화를 고르세요.

①　　　　②　　　　③　　　　④　　　　⑤

7 다음을 듣고, 남자의 직업을 고르세요.

① 내과 의사　　② 치과 의사　　③ 간호사　　④ 교사　　⑤ 외과 의사

8 대화를 듣고, 아래 메모에서 잘못된 부분을 고르세요.

To: All Parents
① Re: Flu Shots
When: ② December 19th ③ From 12:00 to 4:00
Where: ④ In the gymnasium
⑤ Shots are free of charge.

Thank you,
Principal Grant

다음을 듣고 빈칸에 들어갈 알맞은 말을 쓰세요.

1

M I _____ _____ this! I missed my bus again!

W _____ _____. There will be another soon.

M I know, but now I'm _____ _____ _____. What if I miss the test?

W Your teacher will probably understand.

M But _____ _____ _____ _____? I could fail the class.

W _____ _____ _____ _____ on yourself.

M If I fail this class, my whole life is ruined!

W _____ _____ _____ _____! Everything will be fine.

2

W Do you _____ _____ stress? Stress has many causes. _____, _____, and family can all cause stress. Stress can _____ _____ _____ on your mind and body. But _____ _____! You can free yourself _____ _____. Try our new DVD, *Yoga for Beginners*. _____ _____ is a great way to relax and _____ _____ _____ stress. And the DVD is _____ _____ _____ _____! So what are you waiting for? Get the cure for stress today!

3

W Mr. Patterson, I won't be able to _____ _____ _____ tomorrow.

M Oh? And _____ _____ _____?

W I have a medical problem, so I need to _____ _____ _____.

M Well, I _____ _____ _____ told me sooner.

W I know. _____ _____ _____ not telling you.

M I _____ _____ from you, Holly.

W You're right. I will try to do better in the future.

M OK. I'll let you _____ _____ _____ _____.

4

W Hi again, Mr. Wilson. How are you today?

M I'm not _____ _____ _____.

W What's wrong?

M I have a bad cough, and it's _____ _____ _____.

W OK. Is that all?

M I also _____ _____ _____ and a headache.

W Hmm. Sounds like another infection. _____ _____ _____ quit smoking, like I asked.

M I know. I'll try again soon.

Dictation

5 M Hello! This message is for Joan Smith. My name is Peter Brown and I'm _____
_____ Total Health Insurance. _____ _____ _____ we can't offer you
insurance at this time. You _____ _____ _____ our physical examination.
_____ _____ _____ inform you of this, and I _____ _____ been
able to help you. If you have any questions, please _____ _____ _____.
The number is 838-555-4376. Thank you and goodbye.

6 ① M _____ _____ _____ your textbook for science class?
W I'm sorry, but _____ _____ _____ your book.
② M _____ _____ _____ to begin the science experiment?
W Yes, let's read _____ _____ first.
③ M _____ _____ _____ for the science test today?
W No, but perhaps we can study together.
④ M I'm _____ _____ _____ in math. Can you help me?
W _____ _____. I'll explain everything.
⑤ M What is your _____ _____, Monique?
W I like science class the best. But I also like English.

7 M I really love _____ _____. I love my job mostly because I _____ _____
_____ people. People of all ages, children and _____ _____, come to
see me, especially if they _____ _____ sickness. I get to meet all kinds of
new people. Sometimes I perform tests, like _____ _____. Mostly, I _____
_____. I take care of people while they are _____ _____ _____.

8 W Have your children had their _____ _____ yet?
M No, I _____ _____ them last month.
W Don't worry. The school is offering _____ _____ _____.
M Really? When can I _____ _____ _____?
W They'll be giving the shots on _____ _____, beginning at 11:00.
M Great! Where are they giving the shots?
W In the _____. If you like, I can take your kids when I take my son.
M How about we go together?
W _____ _____ _____. I'll see you there.

CAN YOU MAKE IT AT 4?

UNIT

약속 제안하기

~하는 게 어때?	Why not ~? / Would you like to ~?
~에 만날 수 있니?	Can you make it at ~?

답하기(긍정)

문제 없어.	No problem.
물론이지.	Sure. / OK. / Of course. / Why not?

답하기(부정)

그러고 싶은데 ~해서 안 되겠어.	I'd love to, but ~.
안 되겠는데.	I'm afraid I can't. / I don't think I can ~.
내키지 않아.	I don't (really) want to ~. / I don't feel like ~.
미안, 안 되겠어.	Sorry, I can't.

Words — Places & Occasions

- anniversary
- avenue
- book signing
- celebrate
- ceremony
- conference
- convenience store
- exhibition
- funeral
- gallery
- show up
- temple

01 대화를 듣고, 두 사람이 기념일에 할 일을 순서대로 배열하세요.

_____ → _____ → _____

02 대화를 듣고, 각각의 동물에 해당되는 내용에 ✓ 표 하세요.

	Tiger	Monkey
Has sharp teeth		
Makes a lot of noise		
Has very pretty fur		

03 주어진 표현을 사용하여 대화를 완성하세요.

Would you like	I don't think	no problem	Can you make it

A Hi. I need to see the doctor sometime tomorrow.

B _____ an appointment in the morning?

A No, _____ I can leave school early.

B OK. _____ at 4:00 in the afternoon?

A Sure, _____. Thank you!

들려주는 내용을 잘 듣고 물음에 답하세요.

1 대화를 듣고, 여자가 토요일에 할 일을 고르세요.

① 가족을 방문하기   ② 친구 만나기   ③ 미술관 가기
④ 집에서 공부하기   ⑤ 저녁 식사 하러 외출하기

2 대화를 듣고, 두 사람이 만나기로 한 시각을 고르세요.

① 9:00   ② 10:00   ③ 10:30
④ 11:00   ⑤ 12:00

3 다음을 듣고, 글의 종류로 가장 적절한 것을 고르세요.

① advertisement   ② notice   ③ letter
④ warning   ⑤ news report

4 대화를 듣고, 여자가 오늘 들를 곳이 <u>아닌</u> 것을 고르세요.

5 다음을 듣고, 장례식에 대한 설명으로 올바른 것을 고르세요.

① 수요일이었다.   ② 집에서 열렸다.   ③ 많은 사람이 참석했다.

④ 여자는 슬퍼하지 않았다.   ⑤ 별도의 의식 없이 진행되었다.

6 다음 중 어색한 대화를 고르세요.

①   ②   ③   ④   ⑤

7 대화를 듣고, 여자가 보고 싶어 하는 것을 고르세요.

① the market   ② the temple   ③ the zoo

④ the beach   ⑤ the jungle

8 아래 일정표에 대한 설명 중 올바르지 않은 것을 고르세요.

Book Fest 2011: Schedule of Events

	Friday	Saturday	Sunday
10:00 - 12:00		Games for Kids	Closing Speech
1:00 - 2:30		Poetry Reading	Lunch
3:00 - 5:00	Opening Speech	Book Signing	
6:00 - 8:00	Dinner Banquet	Concert in the Park	

①   ②   ③   ④   ⑤

다음을 듣고 빈칸에 들어갈 알맞은 말을 쓰세요.

1

W Hi, Daniel. _____ _____ _____ _____ today?

M I have a test on Friday, so I'm studying _____ _____.

W Oh, really? _____ _____ _____ we could meet for dinner.

M _____ _____ _____ _____ tonight. Would you like to go Saturday?

W I _____ _____ _____ _____. I'm going to an exhibition at the art gallery.

M Maybe we can meet on Friday night then.

W Sure.

2

M Megan, are you going to the _____ _____ this weekend?

W I didn't know about it. _____ _____ _____ _____ _____?

M Oh, it will be a lot of fun. _____ _____ _____ are playing.

W Then I am definitely going. _____ _____ _____ _____ go together?

M Of course! _____ _____ _____ _____ there at 10:00?

W I have a few chores to do. _____ _____ an hour later?

M OK. I'll _____ _____ then too. I can't wait!

3

W Would you like to _____ _____ your skills at the local science conference? Just _____ _____ in the principal's office. I hope that many of you show up next week to exhibit your science projects. It's a great way to _____ _____ _____. And if you win, it might help you go to a good university. The conference _____ _____ 8:00, but if you have a project, _____ _____ _____ _____ an hour early.

4

M Hi, Angela. _____ _____ _____ have lunch today?

W _____ _____ _____, but I have so much to do! Well, first I _____ _____ _____ to the gas station and fill up my car.

M That doesn't sound so hard. _____ _____?

W Then I have to go to a _____ _____ for a few groceries.

M OK. Is there more?

W Oh yes. I have to _____ _____ my dry cleaning, then _____ some books to the library.

Dictation

5　W ＿＿＿＿ ＿＿＿＿: This has been a very sad week. ＿＿＿＿ ＿＿＿＿ ＿＿＿＿
on Tuesday. My family and I cried for hours. ＿＿＿＿ ＿＿＿＿ ＿＿＿＿
＿＿＿＿ came to visit on Wednesday. They had ＿＿＿＿ ＿＿＿＿ ＿＿＿＿
to say. They came with us to the funeral on Thursday. Although it was sad, it was a
＿＿＿＿ ＿＿＿＿. Afterward, my father asked, "＿＿＿＿ ＿＿＿＿ ＿＿＿＿
＿＿＿＿ go home now?" But I wanted to stay and ＿＿＿＿ ＿＿＿＿ my family
longer.

6　① M Shall we ＿＿＿＿ ＿＿＿＿ ＿＿＿＿ in the park?
　　　W I think it's too hot outside.
　　② M ＿＿＿＿ ＿＿＿＿ invite your cousin to the party?
　　　W ＿＿＿＿. He's a lot of fun.
　　③ M ＿＿＿＿ ＿＿＿＿ ＿＿＿＿ ＿＿＿＿ to meet after school.
　　　W Of course. Can you ＿＿＿＿ ＿＿＿＿ at 4:30?
　　④ M When would you like ＿＿＿＿ ＿＿＿＿ ＿＿＿＿ our school project?
　　　W No thanks. I already did my homework.
　　⑤ M That sweater ＿＿＿＿ ＿＿＿＿ ＿＿＿＿.
　　　W Thanks! It was ＿＿＿＿ ＿＿＿＿ from my aunt.

7　M It's so great to be in Thailand!
　　W What do you ＿＿＿＿ ＿＿＿＿ ＿＿＿＿ first?
　　M We could ＿＿＿＿ ＿＿＿＿ ＿＿＿＿ ＿＿＿＿ or take a jungle tour.
　　W I don't know. It seems too hot for that. ＿＿＿＿ ＿＿＿＿ visiting a temple?
　　M That sounds kind of boring. ＿＿＿＿ ＿＿＿＿ go to the zoo?
　　W I ＿＿＿＿ ＿＿＿＿ ＿＿＿＿ doing that much walking right now.
　　M Well, shall we go shopping ＿＿＿＿ ＿＿＿＿ ＿＿＿＿?
　　W How about we discuss it ＿＿＿＿ ＿＿＿＿?

8　M ① Friday's opening speech will ＿＿＿＿ ＿＿＿＿ ＿＿＿＿ a special dinner at 6:00.
　　　② Saturday will end ＿＿＿＿ ＿＿＿＿ ＿＿＿＿ in the park until 8:00.
　　　③ Writers will be ＿＿＿＿ ＿＿＿＿ for fans at 3:00 on Saturday.
　　　④ Special children's programs ＿＿＿＿ ＿＿＿＿ ＿＿＿＿ Sunday morning.
　　　⑤ The ＿＿＿＿ ＿＿＿＿ is scheduled before the book signing.

HOW DID YOU LIKE IT?

의견 묻기

~ 어땠어?	How did you like ~?
그게 ~하다고 생각했니?	Did you find it ~?
~에 대해서 어떻게 생각해/생각했니?	What do/did you think of/about ~?
어느 팀이 이길 것 같니?	Which team do you think will win?

답하기

난 ~라고 생각해/생각했어.	I think/thought ~.
난 그게 ~하다고 생각했어.	I found it ~.
내가 아는 바에 의하면 ~.	As far as I know ~.
잘 모르겠어.	I have no idea.

Words · Art & Culture

- compose
- creative
- global
- modern
- painting
- performance
- quality
- religion
- sculpture
- standard
- talent
- technique

01 다음을 듣고, 남자가 설명한 십자가 모양이 <u>아닌</u> 것을 고르세요.

a b c

02 대화를 듣고, 내용과 일치하면 T, 일치하지 않으면 F에 ✓ 표 하세요.

1 The man gave a speech about world hunger. ☐T ☐F
2 The woman will donate food and clothes to charity. ☐T ☐F

03 주어진 표현을 사용하여 대화를 완성하세요.

What did you think of	Did you find it	I thought	I found it

A Hi, Mr. Harris. Did you come to the school play last night?
B Yes, Rosa. _____ very entertaining.
A _____ my performance? _____ exciting?
B _____ it showed a lot of talent. I think you'll go far as an actress, Rosa.

들려주는 내용을 잘 듣고 물음에 답하세요.

1 대화를 듣고, 두 사람이 보고 있는 그림을 고르세요.

① ② ③ ④ ⑤

2 대화를 듣고, 여자의 심정으로 가장 적절한 것을 고르세요.

① surprised ② satisfied ③ unhappy
④ disappointed ⑤ angry

3 다음을 듣고, 남자의 문제가 무엇이었는지 고르세요.

① 작업 시간이 너무 길었다. ② 영감을 얻지 못하고 있었다.
③ 자신이 만든 노래가 마음에 들지 않았다. ④ 이유 없이 기분이 우울했다.
⑤ 악기를 제대로 연주할 수 없었다.

4 대화를 듣고, 여자가 지불할 금액을 고르세요.

① $600 ② $1,400 ③ $1,600 ④ $1,650 ⑤ $1,700

5 대화를 듣고, 대화의 주제를 고르세요.

① The spread of western culture
② Good things about western culture
③ Western TV shows and foods
④ Celebrating one's own culture
⑤ Bad things about western culture

6 대화를 듣고, 남자가 열쇠를 찾은 곳을 고르세요.

7 다음을 듣고, 여자가 The Monsters라는 소설을 출판하지 않기로 한 이유를 고르세요.

① 흥미진진하지 않아서
② 이야기에 사실성이 없어서
③ 스릴러를 좋아하지 않아서
④ 등장인물이 매력적이지 않아서
⑤ 제목이 좋지 않아서

8 대화를 듣고, 상황에 가장 적합한 속담을 고르세요.

① Every cloud has a silver lining.
② All that glitters is not gold.
③ You can't keep a good man down.
④ The early bird catches the worm.
⑤ A bird in the hand is worth two in the bush.

다음을 듣고 빈칸에 들어갈 알맞은 말을 쓰세요.

1

W Oh, I love this painting! It's my favorite. _____ _____ _____ _____ of it?

M I _____ _____ beautiful. I love the big, blue sky and the field of grass.

W I know. _____ _____ _____ is the trees. Look how they are painted.

M Oh, I see. He used a really _____ _____.

W _____ _____ _____ _____ the leaves are blowing in the wind, doesn't it?

M Yes, it really _____ _____ _____ _____ I'm standing in that field.

2

M That piano is beautiful, Grace. Did you buy a _____ _____?

W Yes, just yesterday. _____ _____ _____!

M Which type of piano did you buy?

W I got _____ _____ _____, but the quality is excellent.

M How does it _____ _____ your old one?

W Oh, it is much, much better. I _____ _____ I even play better now!

3

M Being a songwriter is hard work sometimes. This morning I didn't _____ _____. But I had to work anyway. So I sat down _____ _____ _____ and played my instruments. After a while, something I played _____ _____, and I got an idea. That little idea grew and grew. _____ _____ _____ _____, I composed an entire song. I think these are _____ _____ _____: achieving something special when you _____ _____ _____.

4

M Welcome to Johnson Art Gallery. Can I help you?

W Yes. _____ _____ _____ a piece of art for my home.

M What type of art _____ _____ _____?

W A sculpture would be wonderful.

M _____ _____ _____ _____ _____ this one?

W Oh, it's very modern. _____ _____ it's great. How much?

M How about $2,000?

W Hmm, that's a lot. Can you _____ _____ about $600?

M I can't do that, but I can _____ _____ $300.

W OK. I'll take it.

28

Dictation

5

W What did you think of _____ _____ _____?

M I found it really interesting. _____ _____ _____ the writer's point.

W _____ _____ _____ there is too much western culture in the world?

M Sometimes, yes. Fast food restaurants, TV shows, those types of things.

W I _____ _____. It can have a bad effect on local culture.

M Exactly. I like western culture. But not when it tries to _____ _____ _____.

6

M I've _____ _____ _____ again. Can you help me?

W Where was _____ _____ _____ you saw them?

M I was sitting _____ _____ _____. I put them on the _____ _____.

W But they aren't there now.

M No. I _____ _____ _____ a few minutes ago.

W Did you check behind the lamp?

M No, _____ _____ _____ I could've left them there.

W Didn't you sit down _____ _____ _____ to put your shoes on?

M Ah, yes. That's right. I've found it! Thanks.

7

W Dear Mr. Williams,

I'm Betty Green, editor at Thriller Books. I read the _____ _____ that you sent, *The Monsters*. Although I thought some parts were good, we are _____ _____ _____ _____ it at this time. We have high standards for our novels. I think that if you make the story _____ _____, we might read it again in the future.

Sincerely, Betty Green

8

W _____ _____ _____ _____ _____ math class?

M I think it's really hard. Math is not my best subject.

W _____ _____ _____ _____ on the test?

M I failed it. My mom _____ _____.

W So what do you plan to do about it?

M I study _____ _____ every night.

W _____ _____ you really want to do well.

M I try to do everything _____ _____ _____ of my ability.

W With such a _____ _____, things will definitely get better.

DON'T YOU THINK SO?

동의 여부 묻기

그렇게 생각하지 않니?	Don't you think (so)?
～에 동의하니/동의하지 않니?	Do/Don't you agree (with/that ~)?
～에 찬성하니?	Are you for ~?

동의하기

나도 그렇게 생각해.	I'm with you (on that). / Same here. / I agree.
나도 그래.	Me too. / Me neither. / So do I. / Neither do I.
좋은 지적이야.	That's a good point. / That's (quite) right.

반대하기

난 그것에 반대야.	I'm against it.
난 그렇게 생각하지 않아.	I don't think so.

Words   *Nature & Environment*

campaign   climate   control   desert   disaster   endangered

hunt   nuclear   pollution   protect   species   wildlife

01 대화를 듣고, 여자가 휴가를 보내려고 하는 곳을 고르세요.

02 대화를 듣고, 내용과 일치하는 것을 고르세요.

a The man likes having fun activities close to home.

b The woman thinks the country is exciting.

03 주어진 표현을 사용하여 대화를 완성하세요.

Do you agree	That's a good point	I don't think so
I'm against it	Are you for	

A _____ that driving less will cause less pollution?

B Actually, _____. The real polluters are the factories, in my opinion.

A _____. _____ changing the law to make cars smaller and cleaner?

B No, _____. I think people should be able to drive the car they want.

들려주는 내용을 잘 듣고 물음에 답하세요.

1 다음 중 어색한 대화를 고르세요.

①   ②   ③   ④   ⑤

2 대화를 듣고, 대화의 주제로 가장 적절한 것을 고르세요.

① 온실 가스를 발생시키는 화석 연료   ② 대기 오염이 건강에 미치는 영향
③ 환절기에 발생하는 큰 일교차   ④ 지구 온난화와 기후 변화
⑤ 도시와 시골의 기후 차이

3 대화를 듣고, 사냥에 대한 여자의 의견으로 가장 적절한 것을 고르세요.

① 목적이 무엇이든 사냥은 나쁘다.   ② 고기를 얻기 위해서는 사냥을 해도 된다.
③ 새와 사슴은 사냥하지 말아야 한다.   ④ 경우에 따라 사냥이 이로울 수도 있다.
⑤ 법으로 허용된 곳에서만 이루어져야 한다.

4 다음을 듣고, 아래 메모에서 잘못된 부분을 고르세요.

① TO: Sue
     FROM: Mike
② WHAT: Lunch date
③ WHEN: 1:00 on Thursday
④ WHERE: Max's Seafood
     EMAIL: mikeroberts@email.net
⑤ PHONE: 678-555-2567

5 다음을 듣고, 남자가 하는 말의 목적으로 가장 적절한 것을 고르세요.

① 시험 범위를 알려주려고   ② 새로운 과제를 내주려고

③ 앞으로 배울 내용을 소개하려고   ④ 과제를 잘 해온 학생을 칭찬하려고

⑤ 학생들을 재미있게 하려고

6 대화를 듣고, 아래 전단지에서 대화의 내용과 일치하지 <u>않는</u> 부분을 고르세요.

Plant a Tree, Save the Earth!

More city trees means less pollution in the air!!

① Come to City Park and help us plant trees!
② Tuesday, May 10th
③ 9:00 a.m.
④ Meet at the Park Entrance
⑤ Free food and drinks for everyone!

7 다음을 듣고, 글의 종류로 가장 적절한 것을 고르세요.

① speech   ② news   ③ diary
④ novel   ⑤ essay

8 대화를 듣고, 대화에서 언급되지 <u>않은</u> 것을 고르세요.

① solar power   ② burning coal   ③ water dams
④ heating oil   ⑤ nuclear energy

다음을 듣고 빈칸에 들어갈 알맞은 말을 쓰세요.

1 ① W _____ _____ _____ the mayor's speech yesterday?

M Yes. He talked about his campaign to _____ _____.

② M We should probably _____ _____ _____ with our homework.

W _____ _____. I don't understand the directions at all.

③ W _____ _____ _____ the law about keeping pets on leashes?

M Yes. I think it is good for _____ _____.

④ M I think the mountains are lovely in the fall.

W _____ _____ _____. I don't care for hiking.

⑤ W _____ _____ _____ with the teacher about your test score?

M I think _____ _____. But I'm not going to argue about it.

2 W It is awfully hot outside, _____ _____ _____?

M I'm with you _____ _____. Maybe it's global warming.

W It may _____ _____ _____, but I think it's just a heat wave.

M But what about all the pollution? It can cause a greenhouse effect.

W Hmm. _____ _____ _____ about that.

M And more natural disasters, like hurricanes.

W _____ _____ _____ that means the whole climate is changing.

3 M I think _____ _____ _____ to hunt animals.

W Really? So you think birds and deer _____ _____ _____?

M Well, yes. They can't defend themselves. _____ _____ _____?

W That's a _____ _____. But I think hunting can be good.

M Really? _____ _____?

W When the population of game animals is too high.

M _____ _____ _____ _____. It might help control the population.

W So, I guess _____ _____ _____. But only sometimes.

4 M Hello, Sue. This is Mike from school. I want to remind you of our lunch date _____ _____. I think we should go to Max's Seafood. _____ _____ _____? It's the nicest restaurant in this neighborhood. I'll be really busy all morning. So if it's OK, let's meet at _____. Let me know if there are any problems. Call me at 678-555-_____. Thanks!

Dictation

5

M Listen up, class. Today I am giving you some _____ _____ _____. In this class we talk a lot about the _____. We also talk about how _____ can hurt the environment. For your _____, I want you to write a _____. I want you to study how pollution affects our water. _____ _____ _____ all contain pollution, and this puts us in danger, _____ _____ _____? In your report, tell me how we can _____ our water _____ pollution.

6

W Are you _____ _____ _____ trees at Central Park? I think it might be fun.

M _____ _____. It's also great for pollution. That's on Tuesday, May 10th, right?

W That's right. _____ _____ _____ _____ then?

M It begins at 9:00, and everyone is meeting at the _____ _____.

W Great. How about going to lunch afterward?

M Lunch will be _____ at the event.

W That's _____ _____. I guess I'll see you in the morning.

M Yes, I'll see you at Central Park at 9:00.

7

W Disaster struck our city yesterday because of a giant rainstorm. The result was a _____ bigger than any we've seen before. _____ _____, over 100 houses have been destroyed. Three people have _____ _____ _____ and many more are still missing. The flood waters rose during the night. Many days of _____ _____ resulted in the flooding of the river. We urge everyone _____ _____ _____, and to stay away from dangerous areas. We'll be giving you the _____ _____ as they become available.

8

W Class, can anyone tell me where _____ comes from?

M It comes from _____ _____.

W That's quite right. But that's not the only thing.

M Well, there's also _____ _____.

W What can you tell me about that?

M It's _____ than coal, but it's kind of _____.

W True. Did you also know that water gives us electricity?

M Oh yes! There are _____ _____ in dams, right?

W Exactly. This is _____ _____ _____.

M What about the _____? Can't it also make electricity?

W Yes. That is what we call "_____ _____."

VI CONGRATULATIONS!

U N I T

축하하기

| (~을) 축하해! | Congratulations (on ~)! |
| 생일 축하해! | Happy birthday (to you)! |

감사 표현하기

~해주니 고마워.	It is nice of you to ~.
정말 친절하구나.	That's very nice of you. / How nice (of you)!
(정말) 고맙게 생각해.	I (really) appreciate it.
네가 좋아하니 기뻐.	I'm glad you like it.

Words   *Sports & Competitions*

- annual
- beat
- defeat
- final
- injury
- international
- opponent
- rival
- race
- score
- sportsmanship
- victory

01 대화를 듣고, 상황을 가장 잘 나타낸 그림을 고르세요.

02 대화를 듣고, 여자가 야구 경기에 도착할 시각을 고르세요.

03 주어진 표현을 사용하여 대화를 완성하세요.

it was nice of you	Congratulations on	I appreciate	I was glad

A _____ your final exam. You got the best score in the class.
B Well, _____ to help me study, Mrs. Burns.
A Of course. _____ to help out.
B It was really great of you. _____ your time.

들려주는 내용을 잘 듣고 물음에 답하세요.

1 대화를 듣고, 남자의 현재 상태를 나타낸 그림을 고르세요.

① ② ③ ④ ⑤

2 대화를 듣고, 두 사람의 관계로 가장 적절한 것을 고르세요.

① parent – child   ② coach – player   ③ player – fan

④ captain – team player   ⑤ reporter – player

3 다음을 듣고, 남자가 조언하는 바로 가장 적절한 것을 고르세요.

① 상대 선수를 존중해야 한다.   ② 친구보다는 적을 만드는 것이 낫다.

③ 경기에서 질 때는 화를 내도 된다.   ④ 경기 결과가 인간 관계보다 중요하다.

⑤ 상대 선수와의 신경전에서 지면 안 된다.

4 대화를 듣고, 여자가 하키를 좋아하지 <u>않는</u> 이유를 고르세요.

① 야구보다 재미가 없어서   ② 경기가 너무 격렬해서

③ 운동 경기 보는 것을 싫어해서   ④ 경기가 지루해서

⑤ 실제로 해본 적이 없어서

5 다음을 듣고, 아래 일정표에서 잘못된 부분을 고르세요.

Event	Time
① Family volleyball game	11:00
② Lunch	12:00
③ Live entertainment	1:00
④ Potato sack race	3:00
⑤ Fireworks show	7:00

6 대화를 듣고, 대학 진학을 위해 여자가 한 일로 언급되지 <u>않은</u> 것을 고르세요.

① 신청서 보내기 ② 에세이 쓰기 ③ 추천서 받기 ④ 인터뷰 하기 ⑤ 좋은 성적 받기

7 다음을 듣고, 글의 목적으로 알맞은 것을 고르세요.

① to reward ② to invite ③ to inform ④ to argue ⑤ to praise

8 대화를 듣고, 아래 포스터에서 잘못된 부분을 고르세요.

① This Sunday
② Beginning at 7:00 a.m.
③ Starting Line: North Tower
④ Finish Line: Freedom Park
⑤ Prizes Awarded for First, Second, and Third Place!

다음을 듣고 빈칸에 들어갈 알맞은 말을 쓰세요.

1

W Hi, Greg. _____ _____ _____ _____ today?

M A little better. My leg _____ _____, though.

W Yes, I heard _____ _____ _____ in the basketball game.

M Yeah. Now I have _____ _____, and I have to walk on _____.

W I'm so sorry! I hope you feel better soon.

M Thanks. I _____ _____ _____ get back on the court!

2

M Are you _____ _____ the game tonight?

W I sure am. I can't wait to _____ _____ _____!

M Great. As team captain, you have a big responsibility.

W I know, but I'm ready to _____ _____ _____ to victory.

M Just remember everything I taught you.

W _____ _____ _____ your guidance.

M _____ _____ _____. Just get out there and win!

3

M Let me tell you kids an important lesson. Any time you _____ _____ other people, it is important to have good sportsmanship. I used to have a _____ _____ about losing at sports. I _____ _____ _____ _____ my opponent and sometimes shouted and argued. Then, I realized that it's better to treat others _____ _____. Instead of getting mad, now I am always nice _____ _____ _____, even if they beat me at something. _____ _____ _____ an enemy, I make a new friend.

4

W _____ _____ at the last hockey game, James. It was fun watching you.

M That's really _____ _____ _____ _____ _____. Do you like hockey?

W It isn't my _____ _____, actually. I prefer baseball.

M But hockey is so exciting! _____ _____ _____ like about it?

W It's _____ violent, with _____ _____ _____. I just like quieter games.

5

M Welcome to the 10th annual community picnic! _____ _____ _____ _____ of you all to come out for a fun day together. Let me _____ you that there is a schedule of events posted near the picnic tables. At 11:00 we will be having

Dictation

a _____ _____. At 12:00, we are serving lunch, followed by live entertainment at 2:00. At 3:00, join the potato sack _____! Finally, stay late to watch some fireworks at 7:00!

6

M _____ _____ getting into university, Jane.

W _____ _____ _____ _____ to say. It took a lot of hard work.

M Really? What did you have to do?

W Well, first I _____ _____ _____ applications to many universities.

M And then?

W I had my teachers write letters to recommend me.

M Oh, _____ _____ _____ _____.

W It was. Then, I had to write several essays. Then I had to _____ at some of the schools.

M Wow, that does sound like hard work.

7

W Dear Mr. Kim,

First of all, congratulations _____ _____ your school science fair. It's always great to find _____ _____ _____ so interested in science. We were very impressed _____ _____ _____. We would like to _____ _____ _____ _____ in this year's International Science Convention in Tokyo. Students from all over the world _____ _____ _____ in the event. We appreciate your hard work and hope that you _____ _____ _____.

Sincerely, Jack Wong

8

W Hi, Henry. _____ _____ _____ in the City Marathon last Sunday?

M Yes, I did. I _____ _____ in fourth place!

W _____! How long did it take you?

M About _____ _____. I began at 7:00 at the North Tower.

W And where did you finish?

M We ran _____ _____ _____ _____ Freedom Park.

W Great job! I bet you were _____ _____.

M Yeah, but it was a great experience. Plus, I got a small prize for finishing _____ _____ _____.

VII
U N I T

WILL YOU DO ME A FAVOR?

도움 요청하기

내 부탁 좀 들어줄래?	Will you do me a favor?
내가 ~하는 것 좀 도와줄래?	Would you (please) help me ~?
~해줄 수 있니?	Can you ~ (please)?

답하기

물론이지. 뭔데?	Sure. What is it?
그럼, 해줄 수 있지.	Sure, I can. / I'd love to help.
미안하지만 안 되겠어. (왜냐하면 ~)	I'm afraid I can't (because ~).

도움 제안하기

내가 널 위해서 ~해줄게.	Let me ~ for you.

Words   *Travel*

- abroad
- amazing
- baggage
- budget
- coast
- confirm
- countryside
- domestic
- journey
- native
- passenger

대화를 듣고, 남자가 가려고 하는 곳을 고르세요.

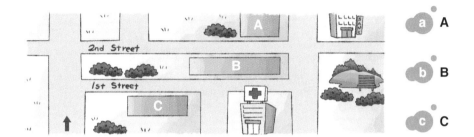

02 대화를 듣고, 내용과 일치하면 T, 일치하지 않으면 F에 ✓ 표 하세요.

1 The man is going to Paris in the summer. T F

2 The woman is going with the man. T F

3 The man asks the woman to buy him something. T F

03 주어진 표현을 사용하여 대화를 완성하세요.

Will you do me a favor	Can you	Sure, I can	I'm afraid I can't

A _____, Meg? I need some help studying tonight.

B _____, because I'm having dinner with my parents this evening.

A That's fine. _____ come over a little later then?

B _____. How about 8:00?

들려주는 내용을 잘 듣고 물음에 답하세요.

1 대화를 듣고, 여자가 지갑을 잃어버린 곳을 고르세요.

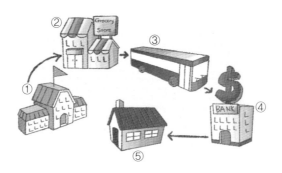

2 대화를 듣고, 남자가 거스름돈으로 받게 될 금액을 고르세요.

> ### MENU
>
> Salad -------------------------------- $3.00
> Hamburger --------------------- $4.00
> Hamburger with cheese ------- $5.00
> French Fries --------------------- $2.00
> Soda -------------------------------- $1.00

① $1.00   ② $2.00   ③ $3.00   ④ $5.00   ⑤ 거스름돈 없음

3 다음을 듣고, 편지의 주제로 가장 적절한 것을 고르세요.

① 사진을 잘 찍는 법
② 여름에 즐길 수 있는 활동
③ 가족과 함께 한 여름 휴가
④ 숲 속의 오두막집
⑤ 기차 여행의 장점

4 대화를 듣고, 대화가 일어나고 있는 장소를 고르세요.

① train station ② bus stop ③ airport
④ subway station ⑤ taxi stand

5 대화를 듣고, 남자가 무엇에 대해 작문을 할지 고르세요.

① 캠핑하기 ② 도시 방문하기 ③ 리조트에서 휴식 취하기
④ 해변에 가기 ⑤ 산에 가기

6 다음을 듣고, 아래 그래프에서 잘못된 것을 고르세요.

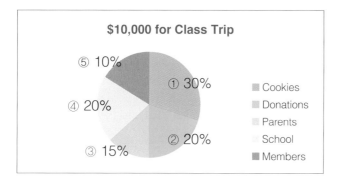

7 다음을 듣고, 글의 종류로 알맞은 것을 고르세요.

① 일기 ② 뉴스 기사 ③ 광고문 ④ 항의서 ⑤ 에세이

8 다음 대화 중 자연스럽지 <u>않은</u> 것을 고르세요..

① ② ③ ④ ⑤

다음을 듣고 빈칸에 들어갈 알맞은 말을 쓰세요.

1

W _____ _____ _____ help me, sir? I can't find my purse.

M Where did you _____ have it?

W I was at the _____ _____. I went there after school.

M And then you came home?

W No, I _____ _____ _____ to the bank.

M Did you have it on the bus?

W Yes, and I do remember _____ with it.

2

W Can I _____ _____ _____, sir?

M Yes. I'll have a hamburger _____ _____, please. Oh, and can you give me _____ with that, too?

W Of course. Would you like _____ _____ _____?

M A _____ would be fine, thank you.

W We have a special _____ _____ today, too.

M That's a bit _____. I'm afraid it's outside my budget.

W OK. How would you like to pay?

M Here is a _____ _____.

3

M Dear Sally,

I am having the best summer ever! We boarded a train and _____ _____ _____ to the countryside. My parents wanted to _____ _____ _____.
So we are staying in a cabin on a lake. It is so _____ _____ _____! But there are fun things to do, too. You asked if I _____ _____ sending you a picture. I don't mind _____ _____!

Thanks,
Michael

4

W Hello, sir. Can you please help me? I _____ _____ _____ to New York.

M When would you like to leave?

W The next _____ _____, please.

M And _____ _____ _____?

W Just one: myself. And I have _____ _____.

M OK. I can _____ that for you here.

Dictation

5

M I _____ _____ _____, Jan.

W _____ _____ _____ help. What is it?

M I have to write about _____ _____ _____.

W Hmm. Don't you like _____ _____?

M I'm _____ _____ _____ the beach.

W Well, _____ _____ _____. Or going to a city.

M I think I like _____ _____ _____ the best.

W OK. Well, write about that then.

6

M Every year, the Spanish students take a special trip. We study Spanish among _____ _____. Last year, we visited Seville. But we need to _____ _____ _____ for this year's trip. Last year we spent $10,000. We got 30% of our money from _____ _____. Another 20% came from _____ from the community. 20% was given to us by the school. 15% came from _____, and the last _____% came from us club members.

7

W Are you _____ _____ the perfect romantic vacation? Look no further than Gulf Island. Relax _____ _____ _____ _____. Watch the dolphins play just off the coast. Eat wonderful _____ _____. Gulf Island has everything you are looking for _____ _____! And _____ _____ _____ you live, Gulf Island is never too far away. A short _____ flight is all it takes to get here. So _____ your reservation at one of our resorts today!

8

① M We could really _____ _____ _____ this summer.

W I agree. How about we talk to a _____ _____?

② M I can't believe we _____ _____ in the city.

W _____ _____ we were able to locate a police officer to help.

③ M Can you please help me _____ _____ _____?

W _____ _____ _____ _____ accept a credit card.

④ M Hi. I'd like to confirm _____ _____.

W No problem. What is your _____ _____?

⑤ M Do you think we should _____ _____ _____?

W I don't think so. It's only _____ _____ _____.

VIII WHY DO YOU THINK SO?

이유 묻기

왜 ~라고 생각하니?	Why do you think ~?
왜 그렇게 말하니?	Why do you say so[that]?
왜 그렇게 생각하니/말하니?	What makes you think[say] so?
~한 이유를 말해줄 수 있니?	Can you tell me (the reason) why ~?

답하기

~하기 때문이야.	(It's) Because ~.
그게 ~한 이유야.	That's why ~.

Words   *Jobs & Career*

- author
- barber
- critic
- expert
- florist
- journalist
- judge
- mayor
- priest
- professor
- secretary
- soldier

01 다음 그림의 상황을 가장 잘 설명하는 것을 고르세요.

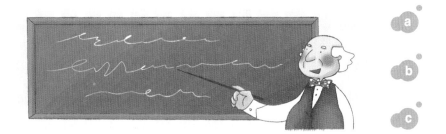

 02 대화를 듣고, 각 직업에 대한 설명으로 옳은 것에 ✓ 표 하세요.

	Judge	Professor
Respected		
Very smart		
Important		

03 주어진 표현을 사용하여 대화를 완성하세요.

That's why	Because
Can you tell me why	What makes you say

A _____ you decided to become an author?

B Well, I love telling stories. _____ I write books.

A I think it's hard to become a writer nowadays.

B _____ that?

A _____ people are buying and reading fewer books these days.

들려주는 내용을 잘 듣고 물음에 답하세요.

1 대화를 듣고, 남자가 여자에게 추천하는 직업을 고르세요.

①　②　③　④　⑤

2 다음을 듣고, 글의 종류로 가장 적절한 것을 고르세요.

① 광고문　② 뉴스 기사　③ 소설
④ 편지　⑤ 연설문

3 다음을 듣고, 여자의 조언으로 가장 적절한 것을 고르세요.

① Study journalism　② Go to school　③ Watch movies
④ Write news stories　⑤ Read a newspaper

4 대화를 듣고, 남자의 심정으로 가장 적절한 것을 고르세요.

① sad　② excited　③ angry
④ nervous　⑤ happy

5 대화를 듣고, 여자가 오늘 가장 마지막에 할 일을 고르세요.

① Order cake from bakery
② Have lunch with John
③ Pick up steak at the butcher's
④ Pick up Dad at the airport
⑤ Go to grocery store to buy flowers

6 다음을 듣고, 남자의 직업으로 적절한 것을 고르세요.

① priest　　　　　② teacher　　　　　③ professor
④ doctor　　　　　⑤ secretary

7 다음 대화 중 어색한 것을 고르세요.

①　　　　　②　　　　　③　　　　　④　　　　　⑤

8 대화를 듣고, 상황에 가장 잘 어울리는 속담을 고르세요.

① All that glitters is not gold.　　② Haste makes waste.
③ A good man is hard to find.　　④ Fortune favors the bold.
⑤ Let sleeping dogs lie.

다음을 듣고 빈칸에 들어갈 알맞은 말을 쓰세요.

1

W It's so _____ _____ _____ a good career!

M _____ _____ _____ _____ _____, Miko?

W There are so many! How will I ever choose?

M Think about something you _____ _____ _____ doing.

W Hm. I like to _____ _____, like my bedroom closet.

M Maybe you would enjoy _____ _____ _____.

W Why _____ _____ _____ _____?

M They spend all day organizing files, meetings, phone calls, and more.

2

M Ladies and gentlemen, this city _____ _____ _____. You deserve a mayor that will listen to your ideas and your complaints. Someone _____ _____ _____, and will do something about it. And ladies and gentlemen, I am that man. _____ _____ _____ this Tuesday in the election. _____ _____ _____, and we can change this city for the better!

3

W People think it's easy to be a professional _____ _____. I ask people, "What makes you say so?" They think we just _____ _____ watching movies all the time. _____ _____, it's quite difficult to become a professional critic. You have to start as _____ _____ _____, writing news stories. _____ _____ I tell people to study journalism if they want to one day _____ _____ _____.

4

W Hey, Mark. _____ _____?

M I'm going to the _____ _____ tonight.

W But that's going to be fun, right?

M Well, I _____ _____ _____ _____ to get my hair cut, and he totally ruined it. Look at this! It looks awful!

W _____ _____ _____ _____ _____?

M It's too short and it's really messy, _____ _____!

W Well, I don't think a bad haircut will _____ _____ _____.

M I _____ _____ _____! I'm definitely never going back to that barber.

5

W John, today is the best day ever!

M _____ _____ _____ _____ _____, Beth?

Dictation

W My father is finally coming home today! _____ _____ _____ who's been overseas. We're having a party, but there's a lot to do first.

M When do you _____ _____ _____ _____ at the airport?

W At 2:00. But _____ _____, I have to order a cake.

M You should buy him some flowers, I think.

W Yes. I'll do that next, at the _____. Then I'll pick up steak for dinner.

M Sounds great. We're still _____ _____ _____ at noon, right?

W Of course! I _____ _____.

- -

6 M I have always been very compassionate, and I love to _____ _____ people's problems. Sometimes, I can even help them find peace. _____ _____ I love what I do. I had to study a lot to become what I am today. Mostly, I _____ _____ _____ a lot. But all the hard work was worth it. Now I _____ _____ _____ my community and my God every day.

- -

7 ① M I am a _____ _____ _____ at the university.
     W Wow. You must be an _____ _____ _____ _____.
   ② W We should _____ _____ _____ about all the noise outside.
     M No, I think firemen have _____ _____ _____.
   ③ M Why do you think people like _____ _____?
     W Some people just like _____ _____ _____ sometimes.
   ④ W I don't understand the _____ _____ _____ _____.
     M _____ _____. I can explain it to you later.
   ⑤ M Traffic is really bad _____ _____ _____ today.
     W _____ _____ I am taking the subway instead.

- -

8 M When I grow up, I'm going to _____ _____ _____.

W _____ _____ _____ _____ _____ you want to do that?

M Astronauts get to travel in space. They are so brave.

W It's difficult to _____ _____ _____.

M Yes, it is. _____ _____ _____ I am already making plans.

W It's also somewhat dangerous.

M _____ _____ _____. I have the courage to face danger.

W Well, _____ _____ _____ to you!

IX PLEASE LET ME TRY.

불만 말하기

어제 이 ~을 샀는데 문제가 있어요.	I bought this ~ yesterday, but it ~.
~에 대해 불만을 제기하고 싶습니다.	I want to complain about ~.
왜 ~하는지 이해할 수가 없군요.	I can't understand why ~.
~하실 수는 없어요. (너무하시네요.)	You can't possibly ~.

설득하기

제가 한번 해 보겠습니다.	Please let me try.
이렇게 해 보죠.	Let's try this. / Let's do it this way.

Words   *Technology*

- advance
- aircraft
- artificial
- automatic
- capacity
- device
- electronic
- feature
- fuel
- gas/gasoline
- scientific

01 다음 그림의 상황에 가장 잘 어울리는 대화를 고르세요.

02 대화를 듣고, 내용과 일치하면 T, 일치하지 않으면 F에 ✓ 표 하세요.

1 The television is older than some others. T F
2 The woman wants a big, flat screen. T F
3 The woman does not want loud speakers. T F

03 주어진 표현을 사용하여 대화를 완성하세요.

| I can't understand | Let's try this | I bought this | I want to complain |

A Hello, _____ about a bad product.
_____ device at your store yesterday, but it doesn't
work.
B Did you drop the product or break it in any way?
A Of course not! _____ why you would ask me that.
B My apologies, but we have to ask. _____, OK? We will
exchange the product for another of the same type.

들려주는 내용을 잘 듣고 물음에 답하세요.

1 대화를 듣고, 여자가 이용할 교통수단을 고르세요.

① train ② bus ③ airplane
④ boat ⑤ subway

2 대화를 듣고, 여자의 문제가 무엇인지 고르세요.

① MP3 플레이어를 살 돈이 없다.
② 새로 산 MP3 플레이어를 망가뜨렸다.
③ MP3 플레이어를 환불 받고 싶어 한다.
④ MP3 플레이어에 음악을 넣을 수 없다.
⑤ MP3 플레이어의 부피가 너무 크다.

3 다음을 듣고, 여자가 광고하는 제품으로 가장 적절한 것을 고르세요.

①

②

③

④

⑤

4 대화를 듣고, 남자가 돌려받을 금액을 고르세요.

① $15 ② $45 ③ $60 ④ $75 ⑤ $90

5 대화를 듣고, 아래 표에서 대화의 내용과 일치하지 <u>않는</u> 것을 고르세요.

Type of Transportation	Price per Day
① Subway	$6.00
② Taxi	$20.00
③ Car	$10.00
④ Bicycle	$0.00
⑤ Bus	$4.00

6 다음을 듣고, 남자의 문제가 무엇인지 고르세요.

① 공부를 너무 많이 한다.　　　　　② 과학을 좋아하지 않는다.
③ 안 좋은 성적을 받았다.　　　　　④ 수업 시간이 지루하다.
⑤ 수학을 잘 못 한다.

7 다음을 듣고, 여자의 조언으로 가장 적절한 것을 고르세요.

① Try to be on time for the final exams.　② Get plenty of sleep and a good breakfast.
③ Study hard to get ready for the test.　④ Tell your parents about final exams.
⑤ Advance to the next grade level.

8 대화를 듣고, 마지막에 들려주는 질문에 답하세요.

①　　　　　②　　　　　③　　　　　④　　　　　⑤

다음을 듣고 빈칸에 들어갈 알맞은 말을 쓰세요.

1

W I'm _____ _____ California on Tuesday.

M I hope you have fun. Are you _____ _____?

W No, there is a short stopover. I _____ _____ _____.

M Well, it's a long way. Maybe it needs to land and _____ _____ _____.

W I guess you're right. Something that big probably needs _____ _____

_____ _____.

M Yeah. Don't worry about it. I'm sure it won't _____ _____.

2

W I bought this MP3 player, but it _____ _____ _____.

M Have you tried _____ _____ _____?

W Yes, but they are kind of _____ _____ _____.

M What is the problem exactly?

W I can't _____ _____ from my computer.

M _____ _____ _____ _____. I have my own MP3 player at home.
Oh, I see the problem. It has _____ _____ _____.

W What do you mean?

M It can hold _____ _____ 500 songs, but no more.

3

W Cleaning house can be _____ _____ _____ sometimes, especially
when you have to _____ and _____ all the floors. Now, there's a _____
_____ _____ keep your house sparkling clean. It's the Zoom Vac! The Zoom Vac
is _____ _____. All you have to do is _____ _____ _____! It rolls
around your house sucking dirt and dust _____ _____ _____ _____. So
if you're looking for an _____ _____ _____ clean your floors, try this today!

4

M Excuse me, I bought a video game from you recently, but _____ _____ _____.

W What is the name of the game, sir?

M _____ _____ "Aircraft Extreme."

W OK. _____ _____ _____. How about you return it for a refund?

M That's fine. I _____ _____ _____, though.

W Just mail it back to us, and we will mail you a _____ _____.

M OK. What about _____ _____?

W We can't refund those, sir. I'm sorry.

M I can't _____ _____ _____. I paid $75 for the game and shipping.

W It's store policy. _____ _____ refund the $15 shipping charge.

Dictation

5
W I _____ _____ why gasoline has to be so expensive!
M I know. It costs me $10 a day just to _____ _____ _____ by car these days.
W What types of _____ do you use now instead?
M Well, the bus is _____ _____ . I can commute for $4.
W How about _____ _____ ?
M It's a bit more. $6 a day is _____ _____ _____ the subway, though.
W Have you _____ _____ ?
M It's too far. _____ _____ _____ at least $30 a day.
W Hmm. What about a bike?
M I guess that would _____ _____ _____ .

6
M Today, we _____ _____ _____ _____ in class. I studied a little bit, but _____ _____ _____ . After all, science is my _____ _____ . I love reading about science _____ _____ _____ . But when I got my test back, I made a very _____ _____ . I didn't understand _____ _____ _____ _____ . I thought I was really _____ _____ _____ . But I guess I'll need to work _____ _____ _____ next time if I want to make the grade. I learned an _____ _____ about being prepared.

7
W This is _____ Walton speaking. I only want to remind students that _____ _____ will be held next week in all classes. _____ _____ these tests, you will not be able to _____ _____ the next grade level. So it is very important that you are ready to _____ _____ on test day. I _____ _____ _____ this: get a full night's sleep and eat a healthy breakfast. That's a good way to _____ _____ your mind is sharp.

8
M I really want to build robots one day. _____ _____ _____ ?
W Yes, robots are interesting. They're so much smarter these days.
M I know. It's called _____ _____ . They think like people.
W That sounds kind of creepy to me, actually.
M I _____ _____ _____ you would think that.
W Well, what if _____ _____ _____ to humans?
M Oh, they're _____ _____ . They only do what they're told.
W _____ _____ . But they might still hurt people _____ _____ .

X UNIT
I HOPE TO VISIT PARIS ONE DAY.

소망/의지 말하기

난 ~하길 바라.	I hope (that) ~.
난 ~하고 싶어.	I hope to ~.
난 항상 ~하고 싶었어.	I've always wanted to ~.
~할 수 있었으면 좋겠어.	I wish I could ~.

계획 말하기

난 ~할 계획이야.	I'm planning to ~. / I plan to ~.
난 ~에 대해 생각 중이야.	I'm thinking of ~.
난 ~할 거야.	I'm going to ~. / I'll ~.
난 ~하기로 결정했어.	I've decided to ~.

Words   *Experience*

- challenging
- happen
- hardly
- have fun
- incident
- likely
- occur
- once
- opportunity
- ordinary
- recent
- valuable

01 대화를 듣고, 남자가 하기로 한 것을 고르세요.

02 대화를 듣고, 내용과 일치하지 <u>않는</u> 것을 고르세요.

a The man might go to the mall.
b The woman wants to come along.
c The man is sure that he is going.

03 주어진 표현을 사용하여 대화를 완성하세요.

| I hope that | I wish I could | I'm planning to | I hope to |

A Trish, I'm having a party on Saturday. _____ you can come.

B Oh, _____, but I can't. _____ visit my family Saturday.

A OK. Well, have fun. _____ see you at the next party.

B Of course!

들려주는 내용을 잘 듣고 물음에 답하세요.

1 대화를 듣고, 대화에서 언급되지 <u>않은</u> 표지판을 고르세요.

① ② ③ ④ ⑤

2 대화를 듣고, 과학 박물관에 대한 남자의 생각으로 가장 적절한 것을 고르세요.

① He is excited to go.
② He likes the old exhibits.
③ He is sometimes bored there.
④ He never wants to return.
⑤ He likes to study science.

3 다음을 듣고, 여자가 장래에 하고 싶어하는 것을 고르세요.

① 학교를 졸업하는 것
② 비행기를 타보는 것
③ 외국에서 살아보는 것
④ 유럽의 도시를 방문하는 것
⑤ 고향 구석구석을 둘러보는 것

4 대화를 듣고, 남자가 여자에게 부탁한 것을 고르세요.

① to buy groceries
② to bring her child
③ to call him
④ to bring food
⑤ to buy a gift

5 다음을 듣고, 남자의 설명과 일치하지 <u>않는</u> 것을 고르세요.

① 유성우는 새벽 2시에 시작된다.　　② 망원경을 가져오는 것이 좋다.

③ 유성우는 자주 일어난다.　　　　　④ Hill Park에서 파티가 열린다.

⑤ 남자는 행사에 참석할 것이다.

6 대화를 듣고, 남자가 가려고 하는 곳의 위치를 고르세요.

7 다음을 듣고, 여자가 보도하고 있는 것을 고르세요.

① 유명한 도둑들　　　　　　　　　② 박물관의 도난 사건

③ 범죄를 해결한 경찰　　　　　　　④ 박물관 행사

⑤ 다이아몬드의 가치

8 다음 대화 중 <u>어색한</u> 것을 고르세요.

①　　　　　②　　　　　③　　　　　④　　　　　⑤

다음을 듣고 빈칸에 들어갈 알맞은 말을 쓰세요.

1
W Did you know that _____ _____ are different all over the world?
M Yeah, I know. I love to travel, so I _____ _____ see them all _____
_____.
W Here in America they are mostly red, _____ _____ _____.
M True. I hear that in Kuwait they also have eight sides, but are _____ _____.
W I traveled to Japan once and saw an upside-down, red _____.
M Interesting. Some _____ _____ _____ in Europe also have triangles, but
_____ _____ _____.

2
M Are you excited about tomorrow's field trip?
W I _____ _____ _____! I love the science museum.
M Me too, but I _____ _____ _____ many times.
W So I guess it's _____ _____ _____ for you now.
M _____ _____. Of course, I do hope to see something new.
W _____ _____ _____ _____. I think they made some recent updates.

3
W When I was a little girl, I loved watching airplanes fly overhead. I _____ _____
_____ on them going someplace exciting and new. At home, everything is _____
_____! Now that I'm older, I have the _____ _____ _____ a little bit,
and I am so excited. Mostly, I want to _____ _____ _____ and see all the
beautiful cities. I _____ _____ _____ _____ when I graduate.

4
W Hi, Bill. I see you're _____ _____ groceries.
M Yes. I'm having a barbecue this weekend.
W That _____ _____ _____. Is it a party?
M Yes. In fact, it's my friend Toby's birthday.
W _____ _____. I hope you have a great time.
M Oh, _____ _____ _____. You're welcome to come, if you like.
W Sure. I _____ _____ _____ this weekend.
M Great. _____ _____ _____, too. There will be lots of kids there.
W I'll do that. See you soon, Bill.

5
M Here's some _____ _____ for you star watchers out there. This weekend
there will be many _____ _____ in the northern sky. It should happen around

Dictation

2:00 _____ _____ _____. Something like this _____ _____
_____, so bring your telescope and enjoy it while you can. Also, there will be an
event at _____ _____ that night to celebrate. _____ _____ _____
be there, and I encourage you to come as well.

6

M Excuse me, ma'am? _____ _____ _____ _____.
W Where do you want to go?
M I need to get to the mall. I _____ _____ _____ my family there.
W _____ _____ _____ _____ of Pine Street and turn left.
M OK.
W At the school, _____ _____ on Elm Street.
M And that's where the mall is?
W Yes. You will see it _____ _____ _____, past Market Street.
M Thank you for _____ _____ _____ to help!

7

W In other news, the famous Grant Diamond _____ _____ _____ from
its place in the city museum. _____ _____ _____ sometime late last
night. Police _____ _____ _____ how the robbers got into the museum
_____ _____ _____. The diamond is the _____ _____ _____
_____, and is very, very valuable. A policeman on the scene said they are
_____ _____ bringing in experts to solve the case.

8

① M _____ _____ _____ _____ go to university?
　 W Yes. I start classes this fall.
② W Why are you packing your bags?
　 M I'm _____ _____ _____ _____ this weekend.
③ M Welcome to Seasons Hostel. Can I help you?
　 W Yes, _____ _____ _____ _____ a private room.
④ W When _____ _____ _____ _____ leave?
　 M We can go after breakfast.
⑤ M _____ _____ _____ _____ climb Mt. Everest.
　 W Do you want to go _____ _____ this weekend?

XI ARE YOU WITH ME?

이해 점검하기

내 말 이해하니?	Are you with me? / Are you following (me)? Do you follow?
분명히 이해했니?	Is it/that clear?
내 말 무슨 뜻인지 아니?	Do you know what I mean?

답하기

알겠어.	I get it. / I got it.
(잘) 모르겠어.	I don't (quite) get it.
이해 못하겠어.	I don't understand.

Words   *Communication*

- accuse
- advice/advise
- agree
- apologize
- argue
- blame
- gesture
- joke
- message
- reply
- rude
- turn down

01 다음을 듣고, 여자가 찾고 있는 고양이를 고르세요.

02 대화를 듣고, 내용과 일치하면 T, 일치하지 않으면 F에 ✓ 표 하세요.

1 The man has a problem with his computer.   T F
2 The woman knows more about the software.   T F
3 The software will fix the problem.   T F

03 주어진 표현을 사용하여 대화를 완성하세요.

Are you with me	know what I mean	I don't get it	I get it now

A It's good to spend your money wisely. Do you _____?
B No, I'm afraid _____.
A All I mean is, be careful how much you spend. _____?
B Oh, OK. _____.

들려주는 내용을 잘 듣고 물음에 답하세요.

1 대화를 듣고, 여자의 심정으로 가장 적절한 것을 고르세요.

① 화가 난 ② 느긋한 ③ 만족한
④ 걱정하는 ⑤ 신이 난

2 다음을 듣고, 여자가 설명하는 수화 동작을 고르세요.

① ② ③ ④ ⑤

3 대화를 듣고, 두 사람의 관계로 가장 적절한 것을 고르세요.

① parent – child ② student – principal ③ boyfriend – girlfriend
④ teacher – student ⑤ parent – teacher

4 대화를 듣고, 남자가 여자에게 당부한 것을 고르세요.

① 두 번 다시 부정행위를 하지 말 것 ② 친구의 부정행위를 눈감아주지 말 것
③ 낙제하지 않도록 열심히 공부할 것 ④ 답안을 밀려 쓰지 않도록 주의할 것
⑤ Monica와 친하게 지내지 말 것

5 다음을 듣고, Helen이 공항 직원에게 할 말로 가장 적절한 것을 고르세요.

Helen	

① Can you find me a later flight?　　② I need to confirm my reservation.

③ I would like to change my ticket.　　④ We should hurry to catch the plane.

⑤ I need a refund on my ticket.

6 대화를 듣고, 남자가 대화 직후에 할 일을 고르세요.

① 친구들 만나기　　② 방 청소하기　　③ 설거지 하기

④ 영화 보기　　⑤ 전화하기

7 다음을 듣고, 아래 메모에서 잘못된 것을 고르세요.

MISSED CALL

① From: Rosa White

② Time: 9:15

③ About: Harry in school

④ Message: Not doing homework

⑤ Call Back: Tomorrow night

8 대화를 듣고, 여자가 남자에 대해 화가 난 이유를 고르세요.

① He did not apologize.　　② He broke a promise.

③ He didn't forgive the girl.　　④ He made fun of the girl.

⑤ He told funny jokes.

다음을 듣고 빈칸에 들어갈 알맞은 말을 쓰세요.

1

M _____ _____ _____ for breaking your computer.

W Don't worry; it's _____ _____ _____.

M Are you sure? I _____ _____ _____ that.

W Well, I have a warranty. That means I can replace it for free. _____ _____ _____?

M Oh, _____ _____ _____. Well, even so, I apologize for being careless.

2

W _____ _____ gives deaf people the power to speak their minds. And when you learn, you'll be able to _____ _____. Today in class we are going to learn the sign for _____. It's quite simple, really. _____ _____ _____ _____, with your elbows down. Then _____ _____ _____ as you would a real book. _____ _____ _____ _____? Great!

3

W Hi, Mr. Wilkes. _____ _____ _____ _____, I need to speak with you.

M Sure. What would you like to talk about?

W Some of the girls at the school have been _____ _____.

M I'm _____ _____ _____ that. Don't _____ _____ _____ you, and they will stop. You understand?

W I _____ _____ _____ _____.

M If you don't react, they'll probably _____ _____ and quit.

W _____ _____ _____. Thanks, _____ _____ _____. See you next class.

4

M Lisa, I _____ _____ _____ this, but I suspect that you cheated on your test.

W _____ _____ _____ _____! What makes you say so?

M You marked the _____ _____ as the student beside you.

W _____ _____ _____. It's probably just an, accident.

M I also know that student is your _____ _____ Monica.

W Sure, but we would never cheat on a test.

M I'll _____ _____ _____ for now. But if I catch you, you will fail the class. _____ _____ _____?

W Yes, sir. I understand.

Dictation

5

M What a crazy morning it was for Helen! She _____ _____ _____ catch an early flight at 8:00, but her car got a _____ _____ on the way. After that was fixed, she arrived _____ _____ _____ to the airport. She found a flight that was leaving _____ _____ _____, so she approached the ticket counter to _____ _____ an attendant. In this situation, what will Helen likely say to the attendant?

6

M Mom, I'm _____ _____ to see my friends.

W Did you clean your room _____ _____ _____?

M No, I'll _____ _____ _____.

W You'll do it now, young man. I asked you hours ago.

M I just don't want to. _____ _____ _____?

W It's your job to _____ _____ _____ _____ your things.

M But why now? _____ _____ _____ _____.

W Because if you don't, I'll _____ you for a week. _____ _____ _____?

M Yes, Mom.

W And don't _____ _____ me again, or it'll be two weeks.

7

W Hello, this is Mrs. White. I teach _____ _____ _____ at the middle school. He hasn't _____ _____ _____ _____ for over a week. If this keeps happening, he might _____ _____ _____. And he may also be _____ _____ for going to the next grade level. _____ _____ _____ _____? Um, the time now is 9:15. I guess I'll _____ _____ in an hour to try and speak with you then. Thank you.

8

M Donna, I want to _____ _____ what happened.

W It was very rude of you to _____ _____ about me.

M I know, and I am very, very sorry.

W _____ _____ _____ in front of the whole class. Why would you do that?

M I just wasn't thinking. You know _____ _____ _____?

W Well, I still don't get it. But I think I _____ _____ _____.

M Can we agree to be friends again?

W _____ _____ _____. Promise never to do that to me again, OK?

M _____ _____ _____ _____.

XII WHAT DO YOU MEAN?

사실 확인하기

네 말은 ~라는 뜻이니?	You mean ~?
그가/그녀가/그것이 ~ 않았니?	Wasn't he/she/it ~?
~ 그렇지 않니?	~, aren't you / don't you? / isn't it?

표현 묻기

무슨 뜻이니?	What do you mean?
	What does it/that mean?
이게 ~의 철자가 맞니?	Is this the right/correct spelling of ~?
~의 철자가 어떻게 되니?	How do you spell ~?
~을 어떻게 발음하니?	How do you pronounce ~?
~할 때는 뭐라고 말하니?	What should I say if/when ~?

Words *History*

- ancient
- century
- decade
- document
- empire
- heritage
- human
- kingdom
- modern
- mystery
- record
- revolution

01 다음 그림의 상황에 가장 적절한 대화를 고르세요.

 02 대화를 듣고, 내용과 일치하지 <u>않는</u> 것을 고르세요.

a Max has a new pair of shoes.
b Max's shoes are ugly.
c The shoes hurt Max's feet.

03 주어진 표현을 사용하여 대화를 완성하세요.

Wasn't he	You mean	What do you mean	didn't he

A _____ on the baseball team last year?

B _____ the guy over there wearing a sports jersey?

A Yes, I think that's the pitcher. He really brought the heat,
_____?

B _____ by that?

A Oh, it means he was a very good pitcher.

들려주는 내용을 잘 듣고 물음에 답하세요.

1 대화를 듣고, 식료품 가게의 위치를 고르세요.

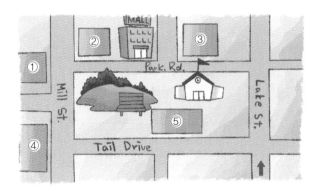

2 대화를 듣고, 대화가 이루어지고 있는 장소로 가장 적절한 곳을 고르세요.

① coffee shop   ② library   ③ bookstore
④ post office   ⑤ police station

3 대화를 듣고, 남자가 선택한 에세이 주제를 고르세요.

① 가족사   ② 스페인 역사   ③ 프랑스 대혁명
④ 프랑스 역사   ⑤ 문화 유산

4 다음을 듣고, 들려주는 내용이 어디에서 볼 수 있는 것인지 고르세요.

① essay   ② story book   ③ newspaper
④ advertisement   ⑤ review

5 대화를 듣고, 여자의 마지막 말에 대한 남자의 응답으로 가장 적절한 것을 고르세요.

M

① I'm not interested in pilots.　② I don't like mystery novels.
③ I'd love to learn more about it.　④ I think she probably crashed.
⑤ I have too many books already.

6 다음을 듣고, Ms. Lee가 지불해야 할 총 금액을 고르세요.

Sales Receipt
Dale's Dry Cleaning

Dress . . . . $2.00 / item
Sweaters . . . . . $5.00 / item
Overcoat . . . . . .$5.00 / item
Blouses . . . . . . $3.00 / item

① $15　② $20　③ $24　④ $29　⑤ $34

7 다음 중 짝지어진 대화가 어색한 것을 고르세요.

①　②　③　④　⑤

8 몽골 제국에 대한 다음 강의를 듣고, 내용과 일치하는 것을 고르세요.

① 제국은 수십 년 동안 지속되었다.　② Genghis Khan은 훌륭한 통치자가 아니었다.
③ 제국의 영토는 아시아로 국한되었다.　④ 제국은 많은 전투를 통해 영토를 확장시켜 나갔다.
⑤ Genghis Khan의 아들들은 제국을 잘 다스렸다.

다음을 듣고 빈칸에 들어갈 알맞은 말을 쓰세요.

1

M Can you tell me _____ _____ _____ the grocery store?

W Of course. _____ _____ on Lake Street. Then turn _____ onto Park Road.

M OK. What do I do then?

W You will pass the city park _____ _____ _____. Then take the next right.

M _____ _____ turn onto Mill Street?

W Yes, exactly. The grocery store will be _____ _____ _____.

M Great. Thanks so much for the help!

2

W Can I help you, sir?

M Yes, I have a _____ _____ _____.

W OK. Would you like to overnight it?

M _____ _____ _____ _____?

W It means the package will _____ _____.

M That sounds fine. _____ _____ _____?

W A bit. You'll need _____ _____ _____.

M OK, I suppose _____ _____ _____.

W We'll _____ _____ _____ tonight, sir.

3

W Have you begun your _____ _____, Simon?

M Yes, Maria. I started last night. It's going _____ _____ _____.

W What does that mean?

M Oh, it's a way of saying _____ _____ _____.

W I see. Well, then my essay will be tough as well.

M I'm writing about the _____ _____.

W That's exciting. I'm writing about _____ _____.

M Your family _____ _____ Spain, right?

W Yes, I want to learn more _____ _____ _____.

4

W _____ _____ _____ _____, there was an evil queen with magic powers. She lived in _____ _____ _____ far, far away from here. _____ _____, she asked her magic mirror, "_____ _____ the most beautiful woman of all?" But the magic mirror _____ _____ _____ there was a girl much more beautiful than she. The queen became angry, and _____ _____ _____ to make the prettier girl _____ _____.

76

Dictation

5

W Do you know the story of Amelia Earhart?

M Yes. She was a pilot, _____ _____?

W She was. She _____ over a century ago.

M She tried to fly around the world, but never _____ _____ across the Pacific Ocean.

W Yes, it's _____ _____ _____. No one knows what happened.

M Didn't she hold _____ _____ _____?

W In fact, she did. The first woman _____ _____ _____ across the Atlantic.

M Wow, _____ _____ _____ a lot about the subject.

W I read a great book about it. I can let you borrow it _____ _____ _____.

6

W This message is for Ms. Lee. I'm _____ _____ Dale's Dry Cleaning to tell you that your _____ _____ _____. You had one dress for $2, _____ _____ for $5 each, an overcoat that cost $5, and _____ _____ for $12 altogether. You can _____ _____ _____ anytime this afternoon. Thanks again _____ _____ _____.

7

① M This is a new car you're driving, _____ _____?

W Yes, I _____ _____ it on Saturday.

② M Jina and I met _____ _____ _____ _____.

W That was more than a _____ _____.

③ M _____ _____ that new painting at the museum _____?

W I don't know. It's so hard to tell with _____ _____.

④ M Is this the _____ _____ of "acheive"?

W Um, no. The *i* _____ _____ the *e*, I think.

⑤ M _____ _____! The robot looks almost like a human.

W No, I don't think most robots are _____ _____.

8

M The Mongol Empire, um, _____ _____ Genghis Khan, covered most of Asia and _____ _____ Europe, too. That makes it the largest in history, _____ _____? It lasted for _____ _____ hundred years. Many _____ were fought to get new lands and keep old ones. But after the death of Genghis Khan, the empire began to _____ _____. His sons could not rule them successfully. _____ _____ _____, the great empire crumbled.

MEMO

Memo

MEMO

10 대화를 듣고, 영화에 대한 여자의 의견으로 가장 적절한 것을 고르시오.

① 액션이 훌륭했다.　　　　② 최고의 영화였다.
③ 내용이 지루했다.　　　　④ 충분히 무섭지 않았다.
⑤ 배우들의 연기가 좋지 않았다.

[11~12] 대화를 듣고, 여자가 남자에게 조언한 것을 고르시오.

11 ① 문제가 풀릴 때까지 포기하지 말 것
② 평소에 수학을 좀 더 열심히 공부할 것
③ 다른 방법으로 문제를 풀어 볼 것
④ 문제를 다시 잘 읽어볼 것
⑤ 너무 어려운 문제는 건너 뛸 것

12 ① Attend the meeting　　② Have his phone repaired
③ Check his messages　　④ Leave a message
⑤ Buy a new phone

13 유령의 집 행사에 대한 다음 내용을 듣고, 일치하지 <u>않는</u> 것을 고르시오.

> ## HAUNTED HOUSE
> **Enjoy a good scare this Halloween at...**
> **the *House of Screams*!**
>
> ① October 31st
> ② 5:00 pm - 1:00 am
> 113 Taylor Street
> ③ Admission: $5
> ④ Admission is half off after midnight!
> ⑤ Discounts for groups of three or more people!

14 다음을 듣고, 글의 종류로 가장 적절한 것을 고르시오.

① 입학식 축사　　　　　　② 합격 통지서
③ 신입생 오리엔테이션 안내문　④ 대학 홍보문
⑤ 등록금 납부 안내문

15 대화를 듣고, 남자가 지불할 총 금액을 고르시오.

① $70　② $76　③ $100　④ $106　⑤ $126

16 대화를 듣고, 남자가 여자에게 권유한 것을 고르시오.

① 점심 같이 먹기　　　　② 공원에서 휴식 취하기
③ 쓰레기 버리지 않기　　④ 자원 봉사에 참여하기
⑤ 함께 산책하기

17 다음을 듣고, 무엇에 대한 내용인지 고르시오.

① 연극의 기원　　　　　② 예술과 과학의 공통점
③ 유명한 고대 과학자들　④ 고대 그리스 문명의 중요성
⑤ 호메로스의 생애

18 대화를 듣고, 여자가 찾아가고자 하는 곳의 위치를 고르시오.

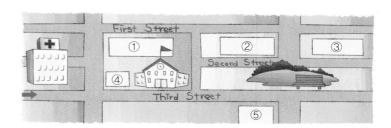

19 대화를 듣고, 언급되지 <u>않은</u> 종목을 고르시오.

① high jump　　　　② 100-meter race
③ 400-meter race　④ relay race
⑤ long jump

20 대화를 듣고, 여자의 심정으로 가장 적절한 것을 고르시오.

① angry　② calm　③ bored
④ excited　⑤ sad

모의고사 3회

01 대화를 듣고, 여자가 도서관에 갈 방법을 고르시오.

02 다음 뉴스 기사를 듣고, 무엇에 대한 내용인지 고르시오.

① 홍수 예방을 위한 노력
② 폭우로 인한 정전 발생
③ 허리케인의 진행과 피해 상황
④ 수재민을 위한 구호 요청
⑤ Florida 연안의 날씨

03 다음 그림에 나타난 상황을 가장 잘 설명하는 문장을 고르시오.

①　　　②　　　③　　　④　　　⑤

04 어제 열린 축구 경기에 대한 다음 대화를 듣고, 내용과 일치하는 것을 고르시오.

① 두 사람이 응원하는 팀이 졌다.
② 한 선수가 부상을 당했다.
③ 경기는 결승전이었다.
④ 경기는 낮에 열렸다.
⑤ 경기는 매우 지루했다.

05 다음을 듣고, 여자가 편지를 쓴 목적으로 가장 적절한 것을 고르시오.

① to thank　　② to complain　　③ to invite
④ to inform　　⑤ to request

06 대화를 듣고, 두 사람이 만날 시각을 고르시오.

① 3시　　② 4시　　③ 5시　　④ 6시　　⑤ 7시

[7–8] 대화를 듣고, 여자의 마지막 말에 대한 남자의 응답으로 가장 적절한 것을 고르시오.

07 ① Yes, I'll take the old lamp back.
② Sure, I can use it to buy a new lamp.
③ No, I don't want a lamp, thank you.
④ I'm never shopping here again.
⑤ Yes, I'd like the same kind of lamp.

08 ① That's true. I'll get a small car.
② I really want a truck though.
③ Actually, some small cars are expensive.
④ I should research electric cars.
⑤ How do you like your new car?

09 다음을 듣고, 아래 스코어보드에서 점수가 잘못 표기된 회를 고르시오.

Teams	Innings								
	1	2	3	4	5	6	7	8	9
Tigers	X	1	X	2	1	X	X		
Giants	X	1	1	X	1	X	1		

① 2회　　② 3회　　③ 4회　　④ 5회　　⑤ 7회

10 대화를 듣고, 내용과 일치하는 것을 고르시오.

① 여자는 정치 분야에서 일하고 싶어 한다.
② 남자는 아직 진로를 결정하지 않았다.
③ 여자는 역사학자가 되고 싶어 한다.
④ 남자는 역사에 관심이 많다.
⑤ 여자는 선생님이 되고 싶어 한다.

11 대화를 듣고, 남자가 전화를 건 목적을 고르시오.

① To make a reservation
② To make a complaint
③ To request a different room
④ To report a crime
⑤ To give a compliment

12 대화를 듣고, 두 사람이 무엇에 대해 이야기하고 있는지 고르시오.

① 좋아하는 음악 장르   ② 배우고 싶은 악기
③ 가장 좋아하는 록 밴드   ④ 어젯밤에 갔던 록 공연
⑤ 도시에서 즐길 수 있는 활동

13 다음 그림에 나타난 상황에 가장 잘 어울리는 대화를 고르시오.

①   ②   ③   ④   ⑤

14 다음을 듣고, 여자가 기분이 좋아진 이유를 고르시오.

① 좋은 성적을 받아서   ② 머리 모양이 마음에 들어서
③ 데이트 신청을 받아서   ④ 숙제를 모두 끝내서
⑤ 날씨가 좋아서

15 대화를 듣고, 남자가 지불할 총 금액을 고르시오.

① $30   ② $40   ③ $45   ④ $55   ⑤ $60

[16-17] 대화를 듣고, 남자의 마지막 말에 대해 여자가 할 말로 가장 적절한 것을 고르시오.

16 ① I don't like festivals anyway.
② Are you free this weekend?
③ I don't have the tickets.
④ I'll be sure to get tickets early.
⑤ OK, we will buy tickets there.

17 ① Well, it was not my best game.
② Sure, I have a match later.
③ I can't. I have another match later.
④ Thanks. That's kind of you to say.
⑤ Hm. You should consider that.

18 다음을 듣고, 남자의 취미가 무엇인지 고르시오.

① 스카프 수집   ② 자동차 모형 만들기
③ 퍼즐 맞추기   ④ 뜨개질과 바느질
⑤ 디자인 잡지 보기

19 다음 짝지어진 대화 중 어색한 것을 고르시오.

①   ②   ③   ④   ⑤

20 대화를 듣고, 상황에 가장 잘 어울리는 속담을 고르시오.

① Better to be safe than sorry.
② Every dog has his day.
③ Laughter is the best medicine.
④ Beggars can't be choosers.
⑤ The ends justify the means.

모의고사 2회

01 대화를 듣고, 두 사람이 기념일에 할 일을 고르시오.

① 　② 　③

④ 　⑤

02 다음을 듣고, 여자가 하는 말의 목적으로 가장 적절한 것을 고르시오.

① 새 전시회의 구성과 일정을 소개하려고
② 지역 예술가들의 활동 지원을 요청하려고
③ 공공 미술관의 건립을 약속하려고
④ 미술관 개관을 기념하고 축하하려고
⑤ 미술관 리모델링 계획을 발표하려고

03 대화를 듣고, 남자가 메뉴에서 선택한 것을 고르시오.

MENU
① Chicken, breaded and fried
② Grilled Chicken
③ World Famous Cheeseburger
④ Grilled Tuna
⑤ Fresh Salad

04 대화를 듣고, 여자의 심정으로 가장 적절한 것을 고르시오.

① hopeful　② forgiving　③ hurt
④ excited　⑤ bored

05 다음 그림에 나타난 상황을 가장 잘 설명하는 문장을 고르시오.

①　　②　　③　　④　　⑤

06 다음을 듣고, 무엇에 대한 내용인지 고르시오.

① 이번 시즌의 최다 홈런 수
② 시즌 첫 경기 내용과 결과
③ Tigers와 Bears의 상대 전적
④ Bears의 우수한 공격력
⑤ 내일 열리는 경기 안내

07 대화를 듣고, 두 사람이 만날 시각을 고르시오.

① 2:00　　② 3:00　　③ 4:00
④ 5:00　　⑤ 6:00

08 대화를 듣고, 여자가 남자에게 조언한 것을 고르시오.

① 함부로 다운로드를 받지 않기
② 정품 소프트웨어 사용하기
③ 컴퓨터 수리 업체에 의뢰하기
④ 컴퓨터를 재시작하기
⑤ 바이러스 프로그램 설치하기

09 다음을 듣고, 여자의 직업이 무엇인지 고르시오.

① cashier　　　　② banker
③ sales person　　④ business owner
⑤ waitress

11 다음을 듣고, Marla가 남자에게 할 말로 가장 적절한 것을 고르시오.

① Hm. Let me think about it.
② Not at this time, thank you.
③ Yes, I will accept your offer.
④ No, I don't want to study art.
⑤ I'm very sorry to hear that.

12 대화를 듣고, 여자가 쇼핑몰을 좋아하지 <u>않는</u> 이유를 고르시오.

① 너무 붐비고 시끄럽다.
② 너무 넓어서 걸어 다니기 힘들다.
③ 파는 물건의 종류가 다양하지 않다.
④ 예전에 바가지를 쓴 적이 있다.
⑤ 집에서 너무 멀리 떨어져 있다.

13 다음을 듣고, 남자가 하는 말의 목적으로 가장 적절한 것을 고르시오.

① to compliment   ② to complain
③ to inform   ④ to entertain
⑤ to congratulate

14 대화를 듣고, 여자가 남자에게 조언한 것을 고르시오.

① 주말에 아르바이트 하기   ② 대중 교통을 이용하기
③ 학업에 전념하기   ④ 중고차 구입하기
⑤ 휴학하고 돈 벌기

15 다음을 듣고, 남자의 요지로 가장 적절한 것을 고르시오.

① 세상의 변화에 재빠르게 적응하라.
② 부모님에게 의존하지 말아라.
③ 졸업하기 전에 일자리를 찾아라.
④ 걱정하지 말고 긍정적으로 생각하라.
⑤ 학업에만 열중하라.

16 대화를 듣고, 대화가 이루어지고 있는 장소로 가장 적절한 곳을 고르시오.

① 쇼핑몰   ② 소방서   ③ 시청
④ 경찰서   ⑤ 교도소

17 다음 짝지어진 대화 중 <u>어색한</u> 것을 고르시오.

①   ②   ③   ④   ⑤

18 대화를 듣고, 두 사람의 관계로 가장 적절한 것을 고르시오.

① waitress – customer
② customer – chef
③ waitress – chef
④ waitress – manager
⑤ manager – chef

[19~20] 대화를 듣고, 여자의 마지막 말에 대한 남자의 응답으로 가장 적절한 것을 고르시오.

19 ① OK. I'll drive you.
② I always take the bus.
③ No, I don't like trains.
④ The subway is crowded.
⑤ Great. I'll see you there.

20 ① No, you shouldn't go out of your way.
② Great. I'm going to the library.
③ Would you like to read the book?
④ Thanks. I can always depend on you.
⑤ Don't be late for the meeting.

모의고사 1회

이름: 점수: / 100 (20문항)

01 대화를 듣고, 상황을 가장 잘 나타낸 그림을 고르시오.

 ①  ②  ③

 ④  ⑤

02 대화를 듣고, 여자가 남자에게 부탁한 것을 고르시오.

① To help her study   ② To find her book
③ To write her report   ④ To lend his book
⑤ To return her book

03 다음을 듣고, 이 글의 종류로 가장 적절한 것을 고르시오.

① 뉴스 기사   ② 일기   ③ 회고록
④ 시   ⑤ 편지

04 다음 그림에 나타난 상황을 가장 잘 설명하는 문장을 고르시오.

①   ②   ③   ④   ⑤

05 다음 뉴스를 듣고, 내용과 일치하지 <u>않는</u> 것을 고르시오.

① 금전적인 문제를 겪고 있는 사람이 많다.
② 많은 가족들이 집에서 휴가를 보낸다.
③ 여행지로 휴가를 떠나는 사람들의 수가 줄고 있다.
④ 집에서 보내는 휴가를 "staycation"이라고 부른다.
⑤ 여행을 가지 못한 사람들은 불만족스러운 휴가를 보낸다.

06 대화를 듣고, 남자가 할아버지 댁에 가기 위해 이용할 교통수단을 고르시오.

① train   ② car   ③ bus
④ plane   ⑤ subway

07 다음을 듣고, 남자의 장래 계획이 <u>아닌</u> 것을 고르시오.

① 대학에 진학하는 것
② 생물학을 공부하는 것
③ 의사가 되는 것
④ 질병을 치료하는 것
⑤ 의학 역사에 대한 책을 쓰는 것

08 대화를 듣고, 아래 메모에서 <u>잘못된</u> 것을 고르시오.

> **MISSED CALL**
>
> To: John Meyers
> ① From: Susan Green
> ② What: Business meeting
> ③ When: Today at 4:00
> ④ Where: Conference room B
> ⑤ Call Back: 555-7634

09 대화를 듣고, 두 사람이 당면한 문제가 무엇인지 고르시오.

① 발표 주제 정하기
② 에세이를 쓰기 위한 자료 찾기
③ 정해진 시간 내에 과제 완수하기
④ 여름 방학 계획 세우기
⑤ 다음 학기 수업 시간표 짜기

10 대화를 듣고, 남자가 지불할 총 금액을 고르시오.

① $400   ② $450   ③ $470
④ $490   ⑤ $500

Answer & Script

센치한 Listening 길들이기

감성 맞춤 내신 공략

내신 만점을 향한 중등 영어 듣기 기본서

- 최신 개정 교육과정 분석 및 필수 의사소통 기능 수록
- 실제 영어 듣기평가와 가장 가까운 문제 유형 및 소재 제시
- 효과적인 1일 학습량 제시
- 다시 한 번 확인하는 Dictation 코너
- 시·도 교육청 듣기평가 대비 실전 모의고사 3회 수록

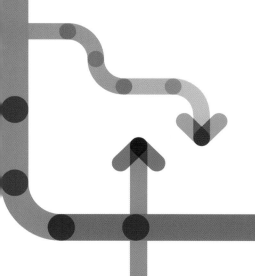

마무리 **1**

센치한 Listening 길들이기

감성 맞춤 내신 공략

마무리 **1**

UNIT I I CAN'T STAND IT.

p.07

Check Up

01 b **02** 1.F 2.T

03 A John, you seem to be angry today. <u>What's wrong</u>?

B <u>I'm getting tired of</u> doing so much work after school.

A I know what you mean. I have a lot of homework, too. <u>I'm glad that</u> the class will be over soon.

B Yes, <u>I'm happy to</u> know that as well. We can both get some rest!

Check Up Scripts

01

M Hi, Judy. You look sad. What's the matter?

W I forgot about our history test. I didn't study at all.

M Oh, no! Do you think you passed the test?

W I probably failed it. My mom is going to be angry.

M Well, I'm sorry about the test. I'm sure you will do better next time.

W You're right. I'll definitely get an A⁺ on the next test.

남 안녕. Judy. 너 속상해 보인다. 무슨 일이야?

여 역사 시험에 대해서 잊어버렸어. 공부를 하나도 안 했어.

남 오 저런! 시험에 통과한 것 같니?

여 아마 낙제했을 거야. 엄마가 화내실 거야.

남 음. 시험에 대해서 안됐다. 다음 번엔 분명 더 잘 할 거야.

여 네 말이 맞아. 다음 시험에서는 꼭 A⁺를 받을 거야.

Vocabulary	history 역사 pass 통과[합격]하다 probably 아마도 fail 낙제[실패]하다 definitely 꼭. 분명히

02

W Good morning, Mark. What's up?

M I have to give a report in class.

W So what's the problem?

M I can't stand talking in front of lots of people. I get kind of scared.

W We have that in common.

M I'm always afraid I'll make a mistake.

W If you like, I can help you.

M Thanks, Beth. You're a good friend.

여 안녕. Mark. 무슨 일 있니?

남 수업시간에 발표를 해야 해.

여 그래서 뭐가 문제야?

남 난 많은 사람들 앞에서 이야기하는 걸 견딜 수가 없어. 좀 두려워져.

여 우리의 공통점이네.

남 난 항상 내가 실수를 할까 봐 두려워.

여 네가 좋다면 내가 도와줄 수 있어.

남 고마워. Beth. 넌 좋은 친구야.

Vocabulary	report 보고, 발표 scared 두려운 have ~ in common ~이 공통되다 make a mistake 실수를 하다 nervous 긴장되는, 초조한

03

A John, you seem to be angry today. What's wrong?

A John. 너 오늘 화가 나 보여. 무슨 일 있니?

2

B	I'm getting tired of doing so much work after school.
A	I know what you mean. I have a lot of homework, too. I'm glad that the class will be over soon.
B	Yes, I'm happy to know that as well. We can both get some rest!

B	난 방과 후에 이렇게 많은 공부를 하는 게 지겨워지고 있어.
A	무슨 말인지 알아. 나도 숙제가 많아. 수업이 곧 끝날 거라서 다행이야.
B	맞아, 나도 그걸 알아서 기뻐. 우리 둘 다 좀 쉴 수 있겠다!

Vocabulary   seem to ~해 보인다   as well 또한   rest 휴식

Actual Test   1 ⑤   2 ③   3 ③   4 ④   5 ④   6 ②   7 ④   8 ④ | p.08

M	Hi, Jill. What's wrong?
W	I can't remember where I parked my car. Can you help me find it?
M	I'm glad to help. Can you describe it?
W	Well, it is a bright blue color.
M	OK. Is it a large car or a small one?
W	It is small and has only two doors.
M	Is that it over there?
W	Oh, there it is. Thanks.

남	안녕. Jill. 무슨 일이니?
여	내가 차를 어디 주차했는지 기억이 안 나. 찾는 것 좀 도와 줄래?
남	기꺼이 도와줄게. 차가 어떻게 생겼는지 설명해줄래?
여	음. 밝은 파란색이야.
남	알겠어. 큰 차니 작은 차니?
여	작고 문이 두 개밖에 없어.
남	저기 있는 저건가?
여	오. 저기 있다. 고마워.

Vocabulary   park 주차하다   describe 묘사하다

W Are computers smarter than people? Some people say yes and some say no. But one computer certainly is. Its name is Watson. In February 2011, Watson appeared on the American game show *Jeopardy*. He competed against some really smart people. Surprisingly, Watson answered more questions than any of the human players! Now that computers can win a game show, just imagine what the next generation of computers will do!

여 컴퓨터가 사람보다 똑똑한가요? 어떤 사람들은 그렇다고 하고 어떤 사람들은 아니라고 합니다. 하지만 한 컴퓨터는 확실히 그렇습니다. 그것의 이름은 Watson입니다. 2011년 2월에 Watson은 미국 퀴즈 쇼인 Jeopardy에 출연했습니다. 그는 몇 명의 정말 똑똑한 사람들에 맞서 겨루었습니다. 놀랍게도. Watson은 참가자 중 누구보다도 많은 문제에 답을 했습니다! 이제 컴퓨터가 퀴즈 쇼에서 이길 수 있으니. 다음 세대의 컴퓨터는 무엇을 할지 한번 상상해 보세요!

Vocabulary   certainly 분명히, 확실히   appear 출연하다   compete 경쟁하다. 겨루다   surprisingly 놀랍게도   imagine 상상하다   generation 세대

3

M	Hi, Mary. I think I have a problem.
W	What's the matter, Paul?
M	I can't go to the Earth Day festival on Thursday.
W	Oh, no! But there will be live music, food, and an art exhibit!
M	I know. I really want to go. I was especially excited about the films.
W	So why can't you go?
M	I have a conflict. I need to study that day.
W	Just study hard on Wednesday instead.
M	Great idea. I'll meet you at Alumni Mall!
W	That's great to hear!

남 안녕. Mary. 난 문제가 있는 것 같아.

여 무슨 일인데. Paul?

남 목요일에 있는 지구의 날 축제에 갈 수 없어.

여 오. 안 돼! 라이브 음악이랑 음식과 미술 전시도 있을 텐데!

남 알아. 나 정말 가고 싶어. 난 특히 영화 때문에 신이 났었어.

여 그런데 왜 못 가니?

남 갈등이 있어. 그날 공부를 해야 해.

여 그냥 대신 수요일에 열심히 공부해.

남 좋은 생각이야. 동문회관에서 만나자!

여 그 말을 들으니 좋은데!

4

W	Good morning, sir. How can I help you?
M	Hi. I have a problem. I need to change my ticket.
W	Sure, I'd be happy to help. What do you need to change?
M	Well, this ticket says I have an aisle seat.
W	Would you rather have a window seat?
M	Yes, thank you. I can't stand sitting near the aisle.
W	I agree with you. I like to look out the window when I fly.

여 안녕하세요. 고객님. 무엇을 도와드릴까요?

남 안녕하세요. 문제가 있는데요. 표를 바꿔야 합니다.

여 네. 기꺼이 도와드리겠습니다. 무엇을 바꿔야 하시나요?

남 음. 이 표에는 제가 통로 쪽 좌석을 갖고 있다고 되어 있는데요.

여 창가 쪽 좌석을 원하시나요?

남 네. 감사합니다. 저는 통로 근처에 앉아 있는 걸 못 견뎌요.

여 저도 그래요. 비행할 때 창문 밖을 내다보는 것이 좋아요.

5

W　Mrs. Smith asked her students how long it takes them to get to school. Then she put some of the results in a graph. Kim said she can't stand riding the bus, because it takes her 30 minutes. John said it takes him 20 minutes. He walks to school, but lives nearby. Jane said it takes her 10 minutes, because her mother drives her. Mark and Bonnie both take the subway, so it takes them both 15 minutes to get to school.

여　Smith 선생님은 그녀의 학생들에게 그들이 학교에 오는 데 얼마나 걸리는지 물어보았다. 그러고 나서 그녀는 그 결과 중 일부를 그래프로 나타냈다. Kim은 버스를 타는 것을 견딜 수 없다고 말했다. 왜냐하면 30분이 걸리기 때문이다. John은 20분이 걸린다고 했다. 그는 학교에 걸어서 오지만 근처에 산다. Jane은 어머니가 차로 태워다 주시기 때문에 10분 걸린다고 했다. Mark와 Bonnie는 둘 다 지하철을 타는데, 그래서 둘 다 등교하는 데 15분이 걸린다.

M	What's the matter, Martha?	남	Martha. 무슨 일 있니?
W	My friend Amy and I had a fight.	여	내 친구 Amy랑 싸웠어.
M	Wow. I thought you and Amy had a great friendship.	남	와. 난 너랑 Amy가 아주 사이가 좋은 줄 알았는데.
W	We do. I just can't put up with her attitude sometimes.	여	좋아. 난 그저 그 애의 태도를 가끔 참을 수가 없어.
M	What do you mean?	남	무슨 뜻이니?
W	Well, I gave her a gift, and she said she didn't like it.	여	음. 내가 그 애한테 선물을 줬는데 마음에 들지 않는다고 말했어.
M	That's not nice. What did you do?	남	그건 좀 안 좋네. 넌 어떻게 했니?
W	I told her she should think of other people's feelings.	여	그 애가 다른 사람들의 감정을 고려해야 한다고 말했어.
M	Maybe it was a misunderstanding.	남	어쩌면 오해였을지도 몰라.

| M | Sometimes I like to volunteer at the local soup kitchen. It is a place where poor or homeless people can get a free meal. I feel like I'm really helping my community. Other times, I like to go to nursing homes. I spend an hour or two chatting with senior citizens. They sometimes get lonely and need someone to talk to. It makes me happy to help them feel better. | 남 | 나는 가끔 지역의 수프 만드는 곳에서 자원봉사하는 것을 좋아한다. 그곳은 가난하거나 집 없는 사람들이 무료로 식사를 할 수 있는 곳이다. 나는 내가 정말 우리 지역사회를 돕고 있는 것처럼 느낀다. 또 다른 경우 나는 양로원에 가는 것을 좋아한다. 나는 어르신들과 한 두 시간 이야기를 나눈다. 그들은 때때로 외로워지고 이야기할 사람이 필요하다. 그들의 기분이 나아지도록 돕는 것은 나를 기쁘게 한다. |

M	Did you watch the royal wedding on TV?	남	너 텔레비전에서 왕실 결혼식 봤니?
W	Of course I saw the wedding. It was the social event of the year!	여	당연히 봤지. 올해의 사회적인 사건인데!
M	It was really beautiful. All the dresses were so fancy. And the hats!	남	정말 아름다웠어. 모든 드레스들이 너무 멋졌어. 그리고 모자들도!
W	I thought some of them were strange.	여	난 어떤 것들은 이상하다고 생각했어.
M	I guess you're right. But the church was really amazing.	남	네 말이 맞는 것 같아. 하지만 교회는 정말 대단했지.

W Oh, yes. It's called Westminster Abbey. It's very old.

M I'm glad that the prince and princess are so happy together.

W I'm sure they will have a wonderful marriage.

여 오, 맞아. 웨스트민스터 대성당이라고 하더라. 굉장히 오래되었어.

남 왕자와 왕자비가 함께 너무 행복한 모습이 보기 좋았어.

여 그들은 분명 훌륭한 결혼 생활을 할 거야.

UNIT II DON'T WORRY ABOUT IT.

✪ Check Up

p.13

01 b 02 b

03 A Dad, I'm the one who broke your computer. I feel sorry about not telling you the truth.

B Well, you shouldn't have lied to me.

A I know. I wish I had told you the truth before. But I was afraid you'd be mad.

B Don't worry. I can replace the computer. But I'm glad that you learned a lesson.

Check Up Scripts

01

M Excuse me. How do I find the hospital?

W Go to the end of First Street, then turn left at the library.

M What then?

W Take the second right turn, onto 5th Street.

M OK.

W The hospital will be on the right side, near the school.

M Thank you. I'm sorry to bother you.

W Oh, don't worry about it.

남 실례합니다. 병원에 어떻게 가야 하나요?

여 1번가 끝으로 가시고 나서 도서관에서 왼쪽으로 꺾으세요.

남 그 다음에는요?

여 두 번째 코너에서 우회전하세요. 5번가로요.

남 알겠습니다.

여 병원은 오른쪽에 있을 거예요. 학교 근처예요.

남 감사합니다. 방해해서 죄송합니다.

여 오, 걱정 마세요.

02

W I love this old vase.

M That's a beautiful piece, isn't it?

W Yes, I love the artwork on it. How much?

여 이 오래된 꽃병 정말 예쁘네요.

남 아름다운 작품이죠, 안 그런가요?

여 그래요. 그 위에 그려진 그림이 정말 마음에 들어요. 얼마죠?

M	Well, it has a little bit of damage on the bottom.	남	음. 아래쪽에 약간 손상된 부분이 있어요.
W	Can I get a discount?	여	그럼 할인을 받을 수 있나요?
M	That seems fair to me.	남	그게 공평할 것 같네요.
W	Oh no! It seems I forgot my purse.	여	오 이런! 지갑을 두고 온 것 같아요.
M	It's no problem. I can hold it for you.	남	괜찮습니다. 손님을 위해 맡아드릴게요.

> **Vocabulary**   vase 꽃병   piece 작품   artwork 그림, 삽화   damage 손상   bottom 맨 밑   discount 할인
> fair 공평한, 공정한   purse 지갑   make a deal 거래하다

03

A	Dad, I'm the one who broke your computer. I feel sorry about not telling you the truth.	A	아빠, 아빠 컴퓨터 망가뜨린 게 저예요. 사실대로 말씀 안 드려서 죄송해요.
B	Well, you shouldn't have lied to me.	B	음. 거짓말을 하지 말았어야지.
A	I know. I wish I had told you the truth before. But I was afraid you'd be mad.	A	알아요. 진작 사실을 말씀드렸으면 좋았을 걸 그랬어요. 하지만 전 아빠가 화내실까 봐 두려웠어요.
B	Don't worry. I can replace the computer. But I'm glad that you learned a lesson.	B	걱정 마라. 컴퓨터야 바꾸면 되지. 네가 교훈을 얻었다니 기쁘구나.

> **Vocabulary**   break 고장 내다   tell the truth 사실을 말하다   mad 화가 난   replace 교체하다   learn a lesson 교훈을 얻다

Actual Test   1 ③   2 ⑤   3 ②   4 ⑤   5 ③   6 ②   7 ③   8 ③ | p.14

M	I can't believe this! I missed my bus again!	남	믿을 수가 없네! 버스를 또 놓쳤어!
W	Don't worry. There will be another soon.	여	걱정 마. 금방 또 올 거야.
M	I know, but now I'm late for class. What if I miss the test?	남	알아. 하지만 지금 수업에 늦었어. 시험을 못 보면 어떻게 하지?
W	Your teacher will probably understand.	여	선생님이 아마 이해해주실 거야.
M	But what if he doesn't? I could fail the class.	남	하지만 이해해주지 않으시면 어떻게 해? 그 수업에 낙제할 수도 있어.
W	Don't be so hard on yourself.	여	너무 그렇게 자책하지 마.
M	If I fail this class, my whole life is ruined!	남	수업에 낙제하면 내 인생은 엉망이 되는 거야!
W	Don't worry about it! Everything will be fine.	여	걱정하지 마! 모든 게 잘 될 거야.

> **Vocabulary**   miss 놓치다   probably 아마   fail 낙제하다   be hard on ~을 좋지 않게 생각하다   whole 전체의
> ruin 망치다   peaceful 평온한   confident 자신감 있는

| W | Do you suffer from stress? Stress has many | 여 | 스트레스 때문에 고통받으십니까? 스트레스에는 여러 |

causes. School, work, and family can all cause stress. Stress can have terrible effects on your mind and body. But don't worry! You can free yourself from stress. Try our new DVD, *Yoga for Beginners*. Doing yoga is a great way to relax and get rid of stress. And the DVD is so easy to use! So what are you waiting for? Get the cure for stress today!

가지 원인이 있습니다. 학교, 직장, 가족은 모두 스트레스를 일으킬 수 있습니다. 스트레스는 여러분의 정신과 육체에 아주 좋지 않은 영향을 미칠 수 있습니다. 하지만 걱정하지 마세요! 스트레스에서 해방될 수 있습니다. 저희의 새로운 DVD, 〈초보자를 위한 요가〉를 시청해 보세요. 요가는 긴장을 늦추고 스트레스를 없애는 아주 좋은 방법입니다. 그리고 DVD는 사용하기가 정말 쉽습니다! 그러니 무엇을 기다리시나요? 스트레스의 해결책을 오늘 구입하세요!

| Vocabulary | suffer from ~으로 고통받다 | cause 원인; 일으키다 | terrible 지독한, 아주 나쁜 | effect 결과, 영향 |
| | free 해방시키다 | beginner 초보자 | relax 긴장을 늦추다 | get rid of ~을 없애다 | cure 치유법, 해결책 |

3

W Mr. Patterson, I won't be able to come to work tomorrow.

M Oh? And why is that?

W I have a medical problem, so I need to see a doctor.

M Well, I wish you had told me sooner.

W I know. I'm sorry about not telling you.

M I expect better from you, Holly.

W You're right. I will try to do better in the future.

M OK. I'll let you have the day off.

여 Patterson 씨, 저 내일 출근할 수 없을 것 같습니다.

남 어? 왜죠?

여 건강상의 문제가 있어서요. 병원에 가봐야 합니다.

남 음, 미리 좀 말해줬으면 좋았을 텐데요.

여 네. 말씀드리지 못해서 죄송합니다.

남 저는 당신에게서 더 나은 모습을 기대해요, Holly.

여 맞는 말씀입니다. 앞으로는 더 잘 하도록 노력하겠습니다.

남 그래요. 휴가를 내도록 해드리죠.

| Vocabulary | medical 의학적인, 건강상의 | sooner 더 일찍, 미리 | expect 기대하다 | have a day off 휴가를 내다 |

4

W Hi again, Mr. Wilson. How are you today?

M I'm not feeling very well.

W What's wrong?

M I have a bad cough, and it's hard to breathe.

W OK. Is that all?

M I also have a fever and a headache.

W Hmm. Sounds like another infection. You should have quit smoking, like I asked.

M I know. I'll try again soon.

여 또 오셨네요, Wilson 씨. 오늘은 어떠신가요?

남 썩 좋지 않네요.

여 어디가 아픈가요?

남 기침이 심해요. 그리고 숨 쉬기가 힘들어요.

여 알겠습니다. 그게 다인가요?

남 열도 있고 두통도 있어요.

여 흠. 또 감염이 되신 것 같네요. 제가 말씀드린 대로 담배를 끊으셔야 해요.

남 알아요. 곧 다시 노력할게요.

| Vocabulary | cough 기침 | breathe 숨을 쉬다 | fever 열 | headache 두통 | infection 감염 | quit 끊다 |

5

[The answering machine beeps.]

M Hello! This message is for Joan Smith. My name is Peter Brown and I'm <u>calling</u> <u>from</u> Total Health Insurance. <u>I'm</u> <u>afraid</u> <u>that</u> we can't offer you insurance at this time. You <u>did</u> <u>not</u> <u>pass</u> our physical examination. I'm <u>sorry</u> <u>to</u> inform you of this, and I <u>wish</u> <u>we'd</u> been able to help you. If you have any questions, please <u>call</u> <u>me</u> <u>back</u>. The number is 838-555-4376. Thank you and goodbye.

[자동응답기 소리]

남 안녕하세요! Joan Smith 씨께 메시지를 남깁니다. 제 이름은 Peter Brown이고 종합 건강 보험에서 연락드립니다. 죄송하지만 이번에 귀하에게 보험을 제공해 드릴 수 없겠습니다. 귀하는 저희 건강 검진을 통과하지 못하셨습니다. 이 소식을 알려드리게 되어 죄송합니다. 도움을 드릴 수 있었으면 좋았을 텐데 유감입니다. 질문이 있으시면 다시 전화 주세요. 전화번호는 838-555-4376입니다. 감사합니다. 안녕히 계세요.

Vocabulary	message 메시지 total 종합적인 insurance 보험 offer 제공하다 pass 합격하다, 통과하다
	physical 신체적인 examination 검진 inform A of B A에게 B를 알리다

6

① **M** <u>Can</u> <u>I</u> <u>borrow</u> your textbook for science class?

   W I'm sorry, but <u>you</u> <u>should've</u> <u>brought</u> your book.

② **M** <u>Are</u> <u>we</u> <u>ready</u> to begin the science experiment?

   W Yes, let's read <u>the</u> <u>directions</u> first.

③ **M** <u>Have</u> <u>you</u> <u>studied</u> for the science test today?

   W No, but perhaps we can study together.

④ **M** I'm <u>not</u> <u>very</u> <u>good</u> in math. Can you help me?

   W <u>Don't</u> <u>worry</u>. I'll explain everything.

⑤ **M** What is your <u>best</u> <u>subject</u>, Monique?

   W I like science class the best. But I also like English.

① **남** 네 과학 교과서 좀 빌릴 수 있을까?

   여 미안하지만 네 책을 가져왔어야지.

② **남** 과학 실험 할 준비 됐니?

   여 응. 우선 지시 사항을 읽어보자.

③ **남** 오늘 과학 시험 공부했니?

   여 아니. 하지만 우리 같이 공부할 수 있을 거야.

④ **남** 난 수학을 잘 못 하는데. 도와줄 수 있니?

   여 걱정 마. 내가 다 설명해 줄게.

⑤ **남** 제가 제일 좋아하는 과목은 뭐니. Monique?

   여 나는 과학 수업이 제일 좋아. 하지만 영어도 좋아해.

Vocabulary	borrow 빌리다 textbook 교과서, 교재 experiment 실험 direction 지시 사항 perhaps 어쩌면, 아마도
	subject 과목

7

M I really love <u>my</u> <u>job</u>. I love my job mostly because I <u>get</u> <u>to</u> <u>help</u> people. People of all ages, children and <u>old</u> <u>people</u>, come to see me, especially if they <u>suffer</u> <u>from</u> sickness. I get to meet all kinds of new people. Sometimes I perform tests, like <u>taking</u> <u>blood</u>. Mostly, I <u>assist</u>

남 나는 내 직업을 정말 사랑합니다. 내가 내 일을 사랑하는 주된 이유는 내가 사람들을 도울 기회를 갖기 때문입니다. 모든 연령의 사람들, 아이들과 노인들이 특히 그들이 질병으로 고통받을 때 나를 보러 옵니다. 나는 온갖 종류의 새로운 사람들을 만나게 됩니다. 가끔 나는 테스트를 하는데 이를 테면 채혈 같은 걸 합니다. 대부분의 경우, 나는 의사들

doctors. I take care of people while they are in the hospital.

을 돕습니다. 나는 사람들이 병원에 있는 동안 그들을 돌봅니다.

W Have your children had their flu shots yet?

M No, I should've taken them last month.

W Don't worry. The school is offering free flu shots.

M Really? When can I take my kids?

W They'll be giving the shots on December 19th, beginning at 11:00.

M Great! Where are they giving the shots?

W In the gymnasium. If you like, I can take your kids when I take my son.

M How about we go together?

W That'd be great. I'll see you there.

여 댁의 아이들은 독감 예방주사를 맞았나요?

남 아니오. 지난달에 맞게 했어야 하는데.

여 걱정 마세요. 학교에서 무료 독감 예방접종을 한대요.

남 정말요? 언제 아이들을 데려갈 수 있나요?

여 12월 19일 11시부터 주사를 놔줄 거예요.

남 잘 됐네요! 어디에서 주사를 놓나요?

여 체육관에서요. 원하시면 제가 아들을 데려갈 때 댁의 아이들도 데려갈 수 있어요.

남 우리가 같이 가면 어때요?

여 그게 좋겠네요. 거기서 봬요.

UNIT III CAN YOU MAKE IT AT 4?

✚ Check Up

p.19

01 c → b → a

02

	Tiger	Monkey
Has sharp teeth	✓	
Makes a lot of noise		✓
Has very pretty fur	✓	

03 A Hi. I need to see the doctor sometime tomorrow.

B Would you like an appointment in the morning?

A No, I don't think I can leave school early.

B OK. Can you make it at 4:00 in the afternoon?

A Sure, no problem. Thank you!

Check Up Scripts

01

[The telephone rings.]

M Hi, honey. It's our anniversary. How would you like to celebrate?

W I don't know. Shall we go relax in the park?

M Of course. But I would like to see a movie afterward.

W Sure, a movie sounds great. What else?

M We could eat dinner after the movie.

W OK. Can you meet me in the park at 5:00?

M It's a date. I'll see you then!

[전화벨 소리]

남 안녕. 자기야. 우리 기념일이야. 어떻게 기념하고 싶어?

여 잘 모르겠어. 공원에 가서 쉴까?

남 좋지. 하지만 난 그 후에 영화를 보고 싶어.

여 그래. 영화 좋지. 또 뭘 할까?

남 영화 보고 나서 저녁을 먹을 수 있겠지.

여 좋아. 공원에서 5시 정각에 볼래?

남 그래. 약속했어. 그때 보자!

> **Vocabulary** anniversary 기념일 celebrate 기념[축하]하다 relax 쉬다 afterward 그 후에

02

W I'm so excited to be at the zoo! What shall we see first?

M Would you like to see the monkeys?

W They are funny. They laugh and scream a lot.

M I would rather see the tiger, I think.

W I'd love to, but tigers scare me. They have really sharp teeth.

M True, but their orange fur is pretty.

W OK. We can see them first.

여 동물원에 와서 너무 좋아! 제일 먼저 뭘 볼까?

남 원숭이 보고 싶니?

여 원숭이 재미있지. 웃으면서 소리도 많이 지르고.

남 난 호랑이를 봤으면 하는데.

여 좋아. 하지만 호랑이는 좀 무서워. 이빨이 정말 날카롭잖아.

남 맞아. 하지만 오렌지색 털이 예쁘지.

여 그래. 호랑이를 먼저 보러 가자.

> **Vocabulary** excited 신이 난. 설레는 zoo 동물원 scream 소리 지르다 scare 무섭게 하다 fur 털. 모피

03

[The telephone rings.]

A Hi. I need to see the doctor sometime tomorrow.

B Would you like an appointment in the morning?

A No, I don't think I can leave school early.

B OK. Can you make it at 4:00 in the afternoon?

A Sure, no problem. Thank you!

[전화벨 소리]

A 안녕하세요. 내일 언제쯤 의사 선생님께 진료를 받고 싶은데요.

B 오전에 예약하시겠어요?

A 아니오, 학교에서 일찍 나갈 수 없을 것 같아요.

B 그래요. 오후 4시에 올 수 있으세요?

A 그럼요. 문제 없어요. 감사합니다!

> **Vocabulary** appointment 약속. 예약 make it 도착하다. 약속을 지키다

1

[The telephone rings.]

W Hi, Daniel. <u>What</u> <u>are</u> <u>you</u> <u>doing</u> today?

M I have a test on Friday, so I'm studying <u>all</u> <u>night</u>.

W Oh, really? <u>I</u> <u>was</u> <u>hoping</u> we could meet for dinner.

M <u>I'm</u> <u>afraid</u> <u>I</u> <u>can't</u> tonight. Would you like to go Saturday?

W <u>I</u> <u>don't</u> <u>think</u> <u>I</u> <u>can</u>. I'm going to an exhibition at the art gallery.

M Maybe we can meet on Friday night then.

W Sure.

[전화벨 소리]

여 안녕. Daniel. 오늘 뭐 하니?

남 금요일에 시험이 있어. 그래서 밤새도록 공부할 거야.

여 오, 정말? 나는 우리가 저녁 먹으러 만날 수 있기를 바랐는데.

남 미안하지만 오늘 밤은 안 되겠어. 토요일에 갈래?

여 안 될 것 같아. 미술관에 전시회를 보러 가거든.

남 그러면 금요일 밤에 만날 수도 있겠다.

여 그러자.

Vocabulary	exhibition 전시회　art gallery 미술관

2

M Megan, are you going to the <u>music</u> <u>festival</u> this weekend?

W I didn't know about it. <u>What</u> <u>will</u> <u>it</u> <u>be</u> <u>like</u>?

M Oh, it will be a lot of fun. <u>Some</u> <u>great</u> <u>bands</u> are playing.

W Then I am definitely going. <u>Would</u> <u>you</u> <u>like</u> <u>to</u> <u>go</u> together?

M Of course! <u>Can</u> <u>you</u> <u>meet</u> <u>me</u> there at 10:00?

W I have a few chores to do. <u>How</u> <u>about</u> an hour later?

M OK. I'll <u>show</u> <u>up</u> then too. I can't wait!

남 Megan. 이번 주말에 음악 축제에 가니?

여 그것에 대해서 몰랐어. 어떤 건데?

남 어. 아주 재미있을 거야. 몇몇 좋은 밴드가 공연할 거야.

여 그럼 꼭 가야지. 같이 갈래?

남 물론이지! 거기서 10시에 만날 수 있니?

여 몇 가지 해야 할 일이 있어. 한 시간 늦게 만나면 어때?

남 좋아. 나도 그때 갈게. 너무 기다려진다!

Vocabulary	festival 축제　definitely 꼭, 반드시　chore 일　show up 나타나다　can't wait 너무 기다려진다

3

W Would you like to <u>show</u> <u>off</u> your skills at the local science conference? Just <u>sign</u> <u>up</u> in the principal's office. I hope that many of you show up next week to exhibit your science projects. It's a great way to <u>build</u> <u>your</u> <u>confidence</u>. And if you win, it might help you

여 여러분의 실력을 지역 과학 학회에서 펼쳐 보이고 싶습니까? 교장실에서 등록만 하세요. 여러분 중 많은 학생들이 다음 주에 (학회에) 참석해서 여러분의 과학 프로젝트를 보여주기 바랍니다. 자신감을 기르기에 아주 좋은 방법입니다. 우승을 하면 좋은 대학에 가는 데 도움이 될 것입니다. 학회는 8시에 시작하지만 (발표할) 프로젝트가 있다면 한 시간

go to a good university. The conference <u>starts</u> <u>at</u> 8:00, but if you have a project, <u>you</u> <u>should</u> <u>be</u> <u>there</u> an hour early.

일찍 도착해야 합니다.

4

[The telephone rings.]

M Hi, Angela. <u>Why</u> <u>don't</u> <u>we</u> have lunch today?

W <u>I'd</u> <u>love</u> <u>to</u>, but I have so much to do! Well, first I <u>need</u> <u>to</u> <u>go</u> to the gas station and fill up my car.

M That doesn't sound so hard. <u>What</u> <u>else</u>?

W Then I have to go to a <u>convenience</u> <u>store</u> for a few groceries.

M OK. Is there more?

W Oh yes. I have to <u>pick</u> <u>up</u> my dry cleaning, then <u>return</u> some books to the library.

[전화벨 소리]

남 안녕. Angela. 오늘 점심 같이 먹을래?

여 그러고 싶은데 할 일이 너무 많아! 음. 우선 주유소에 가서 차에 기름을 넣어야 해.

남 그건 별로 어렵지 않은 것 같은데. 다른 건 뭐야?

여 그 다음에 편의점에 가서 식료품을 좀 사야 해.

남 그래. 또 있어?

여 어. 있어. 세탁물을 찾아야 하고, 그 후에 도서관에 가서 책 몇 권을 반납해야 해.

5

W <u>Dear</u> <u>Diary</u>: This has been a very sad week. <u>My</u> <u>grandma</u> <u>died</u> on Tuesday. My family and I cried for hours. <u>Lots</u> <u>of</u> <u>family</u> <u>members</u> came to visit on Wednesday. They had <u>many</u> <u>nice</u> <u>things</u> to say. They came with us to the funeral on Thursday. Although it was sad, it was a <u>beautiful</u> <u>ceremony</u>. Afterward, my father asked, "<u>Would</u> <u>you</u> <u>like</u> <u>to</u> go home now?" But I wanted to stay and <u>be</u> <u>around</u> my family longer.

여 오늘의 일기: 이번 주는 무척 슬픈 한 주였다. 할머니가 화요일에 돌아가셨다. 우리 가족과 나는 몇 시간 동안 울었다. 많은 친척들이 수요일에 조문을 왔다. 그들은 많은 위로의 말을 해주었다. 그들은 목요일에 우리와 함께 장례식에 참석했다. 비록 슬펐지만 아름다운 예식이었다. 그리고 나서 아빠가 물으셨다. "이제 집에 갈래?" 하지만 나는 가족들과 더 오래 머물고 싶었다.

6

① **M** Shall we <u>have</u> <u>a</u> <u>picnic</u> in the park?
   W I think it's too hot outside.
② **W** <u>Why</u> <u>not</u> invite your cousin to the party?
   M <u>Sure</u>. He's a lot of fun.
③ **M** <u>Let's</u> <u>set</u> <u>a</u> <u>time</u> to meet after school.

① 남 공원에 소풍 갈까?
   여 밖이 너무 더운 것 같은데.
② 여 네 사촌을 파티에 초대하지 그래?
   남 좋지. 그는 아주 재미있어.
③ 남 학교 끝나고 만날 시간을 잡자.

W Of course. Can you make it at 4:30?

④ W When would you like to work on our school project?

M No thanks. I already did my homework.

⑤ M That sweater looks really great.

W Thanks! It was a gift from my aunt.

여 물론이지. 4시 반에 만날 수 있니?

④ 여 우리 학교 프로젝트에 언제 참여하고 싶니?

남 고맙지만 사양할게. 난 벌써 숙제를 했어.

⑤ 남 그 스웨터 정말 멋지다.

여 고마워! 고모가 주신 선물이야.

M It's so great to be in Thailand!

W What do you want to see first?

M We could go to the beach or take a jungle tour.

W I don't know. It seems too hot for that. How about visiting a temple?

M That sounds kind of boring. Shall we go to the zoo?

W I don't feel like doing that much walking right now.

M Well, shall we go shopping at the market?

W How about we discuss it over lunch?

남 태국에 와서 너무 좋아!

여 제일 먼저 뭘 보고 싶어?

남 해변에 가거나 정글 투어를 할 수 있어.

여 난 잘 모르겠어. 그걸 하기에는 너무 더운 것 같아. 사원을 방문하는 건 어때?

남 그건 좀 지루하게 들리는데. 동물원에 갈까?

여 지금 당장은 그렇게 많이 걷고 싶은 기분이 아닌데.

남 음. 그러면 시장에 쇼핑 갈까?

여 점심 먹으면서 의논하는 게 어떨까?

M ① Friday's opening speech will be followed by a special dinner at 6:00.

② Saturday will end with a concert in the park until 8:00.

③ Writers will be signing books for fans at 3:00 on Saturday.

④ Special children's programs will be held Sunday morning.

⑤ The poetry reading is scheduled before the book signing.

남 ① 금요일에 개회사가 있고 나서 6시에 저녁 만찬이 있을 것이다.

② 토요일은 공원에서 8시까지 이어지는 공연으로 마무리될 것이다.

③ 작가들은 토요일 3시에 팬들을 위해 책 사인회를 할 것이다.

④ 일요일 오전에 특별 어린이 프로그램이 있을 것이다.

⑤ 시 낭송은 책 사인회 전으로 예정되어 있다.

UNIT IV HOW DID YOU LIKE IT?

⚙ Check Up

01 a **02** 1.F 2.F

03 A Hi, Mr. Harris. Did you come to the school play last night?

   B Yes, Rosa. <u>I found it</u> very entertaining.

   A <u>What did you think of</u> my performance? <u>Did you find</u> it exciting?

   B <u>I thought</u> it showed a lot of talent. I think you'll go far as an actress, Rosa.

Check Up Scripts

01

M Every religion has a symbol. One symbol is the cross. But there are also several types of crosses. The most common cross is made of two lines, one long and one short. Other crosses include the Eastern cross. It is used by some Christians in Europe. It has one long line which is crossed by three shorter lines. Which cross do you like best?

남 모든 종교에는 상징이 있습니다. 한 가지 상징은 십자가입니다. 하지만 십자가에도 여러 종류가 있습니다. 가장 흔한 십자가는 하나는 길고 하나는 짧은 두 개의 선으로 만들어져 있죠. 다른 십자가들 중에 동방 정교회 십자가가 있습니다. 그것은 유럽의 일부 기독교인들에 의해 사용되고 있습니다. 그것은 짧은 세 개의 선과 교차되는 하나의 긴 선으로 되어 있습니다. 여러분은 어떤 십자가가 가장 좋은가요?

> **Vocabulary** religion 종교 symbol 상징 cross 십자가; 교차하다 common 흔한 Eastern 동부의, 동부 유럽의, 동방 정교회의 Christian 기독교인

02

W How did you like my speech about world hunger, Martin?

여 세계의 기아에 대한 내 연설 어땠어. Martin?

M I thought it was great. I had no idea it was such a global problem.

남 정말 좋았어. 난 그게 그렇게 전 세계적인 문제인지 전혀 몰랐어.

W Oh yes. Many people go without food every day.

여 오, 그래. 많은 사람들이 매일 음식을 먹지 못하고 살아.

M I wish there was something I could do.

남 내가 할 수 있는 일이 있었으면 좋겠어.

W You can donate food or clothes to a charity.

여 자선 단체에 음식이나 옷을 기부할 수 있어.

M I think I'll do that today.

남 오늘 그걸 해야겠다.

> **Vocabulary** speech 연설 hunger 기아, 배고픔 global 전 세계적인 go without ~이 없이 살다 donate 기부하다 charity 자선 단체

03

A Hi, Mr. Harris. Did you come to the school play last night?

A 안녕하세요. Harris 선생님. 어젯밤 학교 연극에 오셨나요?

B Yes, Rosa. I found it very entertaining.

B 그래. Rosa. 정말 재미있더라.

A What did you think of my performance? Did you find it exciting?

A 제 연기는 어땠어요? 흥미로웠나요?

B I thought it showed a lot of talent. I think you'll go far as an actress, Rosa.

B 많은 재능을 보여줬다고 생각했어. 넌 나중에 배우로 성공할 거야, Rosa.

Actual Test   1 ④   2 ②   3 ②   4 ⑤   5 ①   6 ②   7 ①   8 ③ | p.26

W Oh, I love this painting! It's my favorite. <u>What do you think</u> of it?

M <u>I find it</u> beautiful. I love the big, blue sky and the field of grass.

W I know. <u>My favorite part</u> is the trees. Look how they are painted.

M Oh, I see. He used a really <u>special technique</u>.

W <u>It almost looks like</u> the leaves are blowing in the wind, doesn't it?

M Yes, it really <u>makes me feel like</u> I'm standing in that field.

여 오, 이 그림 너무 좋아! 내가 제일 좋아하는 그림이야. 넌 어떻게 생각해?

남 아름답다고 생각해. 넓고 푸른 하늘과 풀이 나 있는 들판이 정말 좋다.

여 알아. 내가 제일 좋아하는 부분은 나무들이야. 어떻게 칠했는지 좀 봐.

남 오, 그래 알겠다. 그는 정말 특별한 테크닉을 구사했어.

여 마치 나뭇잎이 바람에 부는 것처럼 느껴지지 않아?

남 그래. 정말 내가 저 들판에 서 있는 것처럼 느껴져.

M That piano is beautiful, Grace. Did you buy a <u>new one</u>?

W Yes, just yesterday. <u>It is amazing</u>!

M Which type of piano did you buy?

W I got <u>an expensive one</u>, but the quality is excellent.

M How does it <u>compare to</u> your old one?

W Oh, it is much, much better. I <u>feel like</u> I even play better now!

남 저 피아노 정말 멋지다, Grace. 새것을 산 거니?

여 응. 바로 어제. 굉장해!

남 어떤 종류의 피아노를 샀니?

여 비싼 걸 샀어. 그렇지만 성능이 정말 좋아.

남 옛날 것과 비교하면 어때?

여 어, 훨씬, 훨씬 좋아. 심지어 내가 이제 연주를 더 잘 하는 것처럼 느껴져!

M Being a songwriter is hard work sometimes. This morning I didn't <u>feel creative</u>. But I had to work anyway. So I sat down <u>in my</u> studio and

남 작곡가라는 것은 때로 힘든 일이다. 오늘 아침에 나는 창의력을 느끼지 못했다. 하지만 어쨌든 일을 해야 했다. 그래서 나는 내 작업실에 앉아서 악기를 연주했다. 얼마 후에

played my instruments. After a while, something I played inspired me, and I got an idea. That little idea grew and grew. Before I knew it, I composed an entire song. I think these are the best moments: achieving something special when you least expect it.

내가 연주한 어떤 것이 나에게 영감을 주었고 나는 아이디어를 얻었다. 그 작은 아이디어는 점점 커져 갔다. 내가 깨닫기 전에 나는 노래 한 곡 전체를 작곡했다. 나는 이런 때가 최고의 순간이라고 생각한다. 가장 기대하지 않을 때 특별한 어떤 것을 성취할 때 말이다.

Vocabulary	songwriter 작곡가, 작사가 creative 창의적인 anyway 어쨌든 studio 작업실 instrument 악기
	after a while 얼마 후 inspire 영감을 주다 compose 작곡하다 entire 전체의 achieve 성취하다

4

M Welcome to Johnson Art Gallery. Can I help you?

W Yes. I'm looking for a piece of art for my home.

M What type of art do you prefer?

W A sculpture would be wonderful.

M What do you think of this one?

W Oh, it's very modern. I think it's great. How much?

M How about $2,000?

W Hmm, that's a lot. Can you come down about $600?

M I can't do that, but I can take off $300.

W OK. I'll take it.

남 Johnson 미술관에 오신 것을 환영합니다. 도와드릴까요?

여 네. 집에다 놓을 예술 작품을 찾고 있어요.

남 어떤 종류의 예술을 선호하시나요?

여 조각이 멋질 것 같아요.

남 이 작품은 어떻습니까?

여 오, 아주 현대적이네요. 좋은 것 같아요. 얼마죠?

남 2천 달러면 어떻습니까?

여 흠, 비싸네요. 600달러 정도 낮춰주실 수 있나요?

남 안 되겠는데요. 하지만 300달러는 깎아드릴 수 있습니다.

여 그래요. 그걸 사겠습니다.

Vocabulary	look for ～을 찾다 piece of art 예술 작품 prefer 선호하다 sculpture 조각 modern 현대적인
	come down / take off (가격을) 낮추다, 할인하다

5

W What did you think of the news article?

M I found it really interesting. I agree with the writer's point.

W So you think there is too much western culture in the world?

M Sometimes, yes. Fast food restaurants, TV shows, those types of things.

W I totally agree. It can have a bad effect on local culture.

M Exactly. I like western culture. But not when it tries to replace other cultures.

여 그 뉴스 기사에 대해 어떻게 생각해?

남 아주 흥미롭다고 생각했어. 나는 기자의 의견에 동의해.

여 그러면 너는 세계에 서구 문화가 너무 많이 퍼져 있다고 생각한다는 거야?

남 가끔은 그래. 패스트푸드 식당, TV 프로그램, 그런 종류의 것들 말이야.

여 나도 전적으로 동의해. 그건 지역 문화에 안 좋은 영향을 줄 수 있어.

남 바로 그거야. 나는 서구 문화를 좋아하지만 그것이 다른 문화들을 대체하려고 할 때는 아니야.

Vocabulary	article 기사 interesting 흥미로운 agree with ～에 동의하다 point 논점, 요지 western 서구의
	totally 완전히, 전적으로 effect 영향, 효과 local 지역의 try to ～하려고 하다 replace 대체하다

6

M	I've lost my keys again. Can you help me?
W	Where was the last place you saw them?
M	I was sitting on the couch. I put them on the coffee table.
W	But they aren't there now.
M	No. I picked them up a few minutes ago.
W	Did you check behind the lamp?
M	No, I don't think I could've left them there.
W	Didn't you sit down by the window to put your shoes on?
M	Ah, yes. That's right. I've found it! Thanks.

남	열쇠를 또 잃어버렸네. 도와줄 수 있어?
여	열쇠를 마지막으로 본 곳이 어디야?
남	난 긴 의자에 앉아 있었어. 열쇠를 커피 테이블 위에 놓았고.
여	그런데 지금은 거기 없네.
남	없어. 몇 분 전에 집어 들었어.
여	램프 뒤쪽 확인해 봤어?
남	아니, 거기에 두었을 것 같지는 않아.
여	신발 신으려고 창가에 앉지 않았었어?
남	아. 그래. 네 말이 맞다. 찾았어! 고마워.

> **Vocabulary** couch 긴 의자 pick up 집어 들다 check 확인하다 put on ~을 입다[신다]

7

W Dear Mr. Williams,

I'm Betty Green, editor at Thriller Books.
I read the horror novel that you sent, *The Monsters*. Although I thought some parts were good, we are not able to publish it at this time. We have high standards for our novels. I think that if you make the story more exciting, we might read it again in the future.

Sincerely, Betty Green

여 친애하는 William 씨께.

저는 Thriller Books의 편집자 Betty Green입니다. 선생님께서 보내주신 공포 소설 〈괴물〉을 읽어보았습니다. 몇몇 부분은 좋다고 생각했지만 이번에 그것을 출판할 수는 없겠습니다. 저희는 소설에 높은 기준을 두고 있습니다. 선생님께서 그 이야기를 더 흥미진진하게 만드신다면 나중에 다시 읽어볼 수 있을 것 같습니다.

Betty Green 드림

> **Vocabulary** editor 편집자 horror 공포 monster 괴물 publish 출판하다 standard 기준 exciting 흥미진진한
> in the future 장래에 sincerely 진심으로

8

W	What do you think of math class?
M	I think it's really hard. Math is not my best subject.
W	How did you do on the test?
M	I failed it. My mom grounded me.
W	So what do you plan to do about it?
M	I study extra hard every night.
W	Sounds like you really want to do well.
M	I try to do everything to the best of my ability.
W	With such a good attitude, things will definitely get better.

여	수학 수업에 대해 어떻게 생각하니?
남	정말 어렵다고 생각해요. 수학은 제가 제일 잘 하는 과목이 아니에요.
여	시험은 어땠어?
남	낙제했어요. 엄마가 벌로 외출 금지를 시키셨어요.
여	그럼 그것에 대해서 어떻게 하려고 하니?
남	매일 밤 더 열심히 공부하고 있어요.
여	정말 잘 하고 싶어하는 것처럼 들린다.
남	제 능력을 다해서 뭐든지 하려고 해요.
여	그렇게 좋은 태도로 임한다면 분명히 상황이 나아질 거야.

UNIT V DON'T YOU THINK SO?

Check Up

p.31

01 c **02** a

03 A <u>Do you agree</u> that driving less will cause less pollution?

    B Actually, <u>I don't think so</u>. The real polluters are the factories, in my opinion.

    A <u>That's a good point.</u> <u>Are you for</u> changing the law to make cars smaller and cleaner?

    B No, <u>I'm against it</u>. I think people should be able to drive the car they want.

Check Up Scripts

01

W	I'm so excited to go on vacation.	여	휴가 가서 너무 신난다.
M	Don't you think you should pack sunscreen?	남	너 자외선 차단제 챙겨야 하지 않을까?
W	You're right. It's going to be very hot.	여	맞아. 아주 더울 거야.
M	Don't forget your sunglasses, either.	남	선글라스도 잊지 마.
W	I have them right here, along with my camera.	여	바로 여기 있어. 카메라랑 같이.
M	Be sure to take lots of pictures of wildlife.	남	야생 생물을 카메라에 많이 담도록 해.
W	I will. I'm excited to see all the cactus too!	여	그럴 거야. 모든 선인장들을 볼 생각하니 두근거려!

02

M	I would rather live in the city than in the country. Don't you agree?	남	나는 시골보다 도시에서 살고 싶어. 동의하지 않니?
W	I'm with you on that. It's so boring in the country!	여	나도 그렇게 생각해. 시골에서는 너무 지루해!
M	That's quite right. I like the excitement of the city.	남	맞는 말이야. 난 도시의 흥분이 좋아.
W	I like it because there are so many fun things to do.	여	나는 재미있는 할 것들이 많아서 도시를 좋아해.
M	I agree. And they are all so close to my home.	남	동감이야. 그리고 그것들은 모두 내 집에서 가까워.
W	You're so right. I guess we're both city people, huh?	여	정말 그래. 우린 둘 다 도시 사람인 것 같아, 그렇지?

03

A Do you agree that driving less will cause less pollution?

B Actually, I don't think so. The real polluters are the factories, in my opinion.

A That's a good point. Are you for changing the law to make cars smaller and cleaner?

B No, I'm against it. I think people should be able to drive the car they want.

A 운전을 덜 하면 공해가 덜 발생할 거라는 데 동의하니?

B 사실 난 그렇게 생각하지 않아. 내 생각에 정말 공해를 일으키는 건 공장이야.

A 좋은 지적이야. 자동차를 더 작고 깨끗하게 만드는 법에 찬성하니?

B 아니. 난 반대야. 나는 사람들이 자기가 원하는 차를 몰 수 있어야 한다고 생각해.

Actual Test   1 ④   2 ④   3 ④   4 ③   5 ②   6 ①   7 ②   8 ④ | p.32

① **W** Did you hear the mayor's speech yesterday?

  M Yes. He talked about his campaign to stop crime.

② **M** We should probably ask for help with our homework.

  W You're right. I don't understand the directions at all.

③ **W** Are you for the law about keeping pets on leashes?

  M Yes. I think it is good for preventing injuries.

④ **M** I think the mountains are lovely in the fall.

  W I'm against it. I don't care for hiking.

⑤ **W** Do you agree with the teacher about your test score?

  M I think it's wrong. But I'm not going to argue about it.

① **여** 너 어제 시장 연설 들었니?

  남 응. 범죄 예방 운동에 대해 말했어.

② **남** 우리 숙제에 대한 도움을 요청해야 할지도 몰라.

  여 네 말이 맞아. 지시 사항을 전혀 이해 못하겠어.

③ **여** 넌 애완동물을 줄로 묶어두는 법에 찬성하니?

  남 응. 난 그것이 부상을 방지하는 데 좋다고 생각해.

④ **남** 나는 가을에 산이 아름다운 것 같아.

  여 난 그것에 반대해. 난 하이킹을 좋아하지 않아.

⑤ **여** 너는 시험 성적에 대해서 선생님 의견에 동의하니?

  남 잘못되었다고 생각해. 하지만 그것에 대해서 (선생님께) 따지지는 않을 거야.

2

W It is awfully hot outside, <u>don't</u> <u>you</u> <u>think</u>?

M I'm with you <u>on</u> <u>that</u>. Maybe it's global warming.

W It may <u>look</u> <u>that</u> <u>way</u>, but I think it's just a heat wave.

M But what about all the pollution? It can cause a greenhouse effect.

W Hmm. <u>You</u> <u>are</u> <u>right</u> about that.

M And more natural disasters, like hurricanes.

W <u>I</u> <u>don't</u> <u>think</u> that means the whole climate is changing.

여 밖이 너무 덥다. 그렇게 생각 안 해?

남 나도 그렇게 생각해. 지구 온난화 때문인가 봐.

여 그렇게 보일 수 있지만 난 그냥 폭염인 것 같아.

남 하지만 그 모든 공해는 어쩌고? 공해는 온실 효과를 일으킬 수 있어.

여 흠. 그건 네 말이 맞다.

남 그리고 허리케인 같은 더 많은 자연 재해가 일어나고 있어.

여 나는 그게 기후 전체가 변화하고 있다는 걸 의미한다고 생각하지는 않아.

| Vocabulary | awfully 너무, 심하게   global warming 지구 온난화   look ~하게 보이다   heat wave 폭염 |
| | cause 일으키다   greenhouse effect 온실 효과   disaster 재해   climate 기후 |

3

M I think <u>it's</u> <u>all</u> <u>wrong</u> to hunt animals.

W Really? So you think birds and deer <u>shouldn't</u> <u>be</u> <u>hunted</u>?

M Well, yes. They can't defend themselves. <u>Don't</u> <u>you</u> <u>agree</u>?

W That's a <u>good</u> <u>point</u>. But I think hunting can be good.

M Really? <u>Like</u> <u>when</u>?

W When the population of game animals is too high.

M <u>I</u> <u>see</u> <u>your</u> point. It might help control the population.

W So, I guess <u>I'm</u> <u>for</u> <u>it</u>. But only sometimes.

남 나는 동물을 사냥하는 것이 완전히 잘못되었다고 생각해.

여 정말? 그럼 넌 새와 사슴을 사냥해서는 안 된다고 생각해?

남 음. 그래. 그것들은 스스로를 보호할 수 없잖아. 그렇게 생각하지 않니?

여 그건 맞는 말이야. 하지만 나는 사냥이 이로울 수 있다고 생각해.

남 정말? 어떤 때?

여 사냥감인 동물의 개체 수가 너무 많을 때지.

남 네 말 알겠어. 개체 수를 조절하는 데 도움이 되겠구나.

여 그래서 나는 사냥에 찬성해. 하지만 어떤 경우에만이야.

| Vocabulary | hunt 사냥하다   deer 사슴   defend 보호하다   population 개체 수   game 사냥감   control 조절하다 |

4

[The answering machine beeps.]

M Hello, Sue. This is Mike from school. I want to remind you of our lunch date <u>on</u> <u>Tuesday</u>. I think we should go to Max's Seafood. <u>Don't</u> <u>you</u> <u>agree</u>? It's the nicest restaurant in this neighborhood. I'll be really busy all morning. So if it's OK, let's meet at <u>1:00</u>. Let me know if

[자동응답기 소리]

남 안녕. Sue. 나 학교의 Mike야. 화요일에 있을 우리 점심 데이트에 대해서 일깨워주려고. 내 생각에 우린 Max's Seafood에 가야 할 것 같아. 너도 그렇게 생각하지 않니? 이 동네에서 제일 좋은 식당이잖아. 난 오전 내내 정말 바쁠 거야. 그러니까 괜찮다면 1시에 만나자. 무슨 문제가 있으면 알려줘. 678-555-2567로 전화 줘. 고마워! 2567로 전화

there are any problems. Call me at 678-555-2567. Thanks!

주세요. 고마워요!

| Vocabulary | seafood 해산물   neighborhood 동네 |

5

M Listen up, class. Today I am giving you some <u>new class work</u>. In this class we talk a lot about the <u>environment</u>. We also talk about how <u>pollution</u> can hurt the environment. For your <u>assignment</u>, I want you to write a <u>report</u>. I want you to study how pollution affects our water. <u>Streams</u> <u>and</u> <u>rivers</u> all contain pollution, and this puts us in danger, <u>don't</u> <u>you</u> <u>think</u>? In your report, tell me how we can <u>protect</u> our water <u>from</u> pollution.

남 잘 들으세요. 여러분. 오늘은 여러분에게 새로운 수업 과제를 드리겠어요. 이 수업에서 우리는 환경에 대해 많은 것을 이야기해요. 우리는 또한 공해가 어떻게 환경을 해치는가에 대해서도 이야기해요. 여러분의 과제로 저는 여러분이 보고서 한편을 작성했으면 해요. 저는 여러분이 공해가 어떻게 우리의 물에 영향을 미치는지 공부했으면 해요. 시냇물과 강물은 모두 공해를 담고 있고 이것은 우리를 위험하게 하죠. 그렇게 생각하지 않나요? 여러분의 보고서에서 저에게 어떻게 하면 우리가 공해로부터 우리의 물을 보호할 수 있을지 말해주세요.

| Vocabulary | environment 환경   pollution 공해   hurt 해치다   assignment 과제   report 보고서 |
| | affect 영향을 미치다   stream 개울, 시냇물   contain 담고 있다   protect 보호하다 |

6

W Are you <u>coming</u> <u>to</u> <u>plant</u> trees at Central Park? I think it might be fun.

M <u>Me too</u>. It's also great for pollution. That's on Tuesday, May 10th, right?

W That's right. <u>When</u> <u>shall</u> <u>we</u> <u>meet</u> then?

M It begins at 9:00, and everyone is meeting at the <u>park</u> <u>entrance</u>.

W Great. How about going to lunch afterward?

M Lunch will be <u>free</u> at the event.

W That's <u>very</u> <u>convenient</u>. I guess I'll see you in the morning.

M Yes, I'll see you at Central Park at 9:00.

여 Central Park에 나무 심으러 갈 거니? 재미있을 것 같은데.

남 나도 그렇게 생각해. 공해에도 좋고. 5월 10일 화요일 맞지?

여 맞아. 그럼 언제 만날까?

남 9시에 시작하고 모두 공원 입구에서 만날 거야.

여 좋아. 그 후에 점심 먹으러 가는 거 어때?

남 점심식사가 행사에서 무료로 제공될 거야.

여 그거 아주 편리하네. 그럼 아침에 보겠다.

남 그래. 9시에 Central Park에서 봐.

| Vocabulary | plant 심다   entrance 입구   afterward 그 후에   free 무료의   event 행사   convenient 편리한 |

7

W Disaster struck our city yesterday because of a giant rainstorm. The result was a <u>flood</u> bigger than any we've seen before. <u>So</u> <u>far</u>, over 100 houses have been destroyed. Three people have <u>lost</u> <u>their</u> <u>lives</u> and many more are still missing. Many days of <u>heavy</u> <u>rain</u>

여 거대한 폭풍우로 인해 어제 우리 도시에 재해가 닥쳤습니다. 그 결과 우리가 지금껏 보지 못한 심각한 홍수가 발생했습니다. 지금까지 100채 이상의 가옥이 파괴되었습니다. 세 명이 목숨을 잃었고 더 많은 사람들이 실종되었습니다. 여러 날에 걸친 폭우가 강의 범람으로 이어졌습니다. 모든 분들은 이동하지 말고 위험 지역에서 떨어져 계시기 바랍니

resulted in the flooding of the river. We urge everyone <u>not to</u> travel, and to stay away from dangerous areas. We'll be giving you the <u>latest</u> <u>updates</u> as they become available.

다. 가장 최근 소식이 들려오는 대로 전해드리겠습니다.

W Class, can anyone tell me where <u>electricity</u> comes from?

M It comes from <u>burning</u> <u>coal</u>.

W That's quite right. But that's not the only thing.

M Well, there's also <u>nuclear</u> <u>energy</u>.

W What can you tell me about that?

M It's <u>cleaner</u> than coal, but it's kind of <u>dangerous</u>.

W True. Did you also know that water gives us electricity?

M Oh yes! There are <u>power</u> <u>plants</u> in dams, right?

W Exactly. This is <u>clean</u> <u>and</u> <u>safe</u>.

M What about the <u>sun</u>? Can't it also make electricity?

W Yes. That is what we call "<u>solar</u> <u>power</u>."

여 여러분. 누군가 전기가 어디에서 오는지 말해줄 수 있어요?

남 석탄을 태우는 것에서 와요.

여 정말 맞아요. 하지만 그것이 유일한 것은 아니에요.

남 음. 원자력 에너지도 있어요.

여 그것에 대해서 뭘 말해줄 수 있나요?

남 그건 석탄보다 깨끗하지만 좀 위험해요.

여 맞아요. 물도 우리에게 전기를 주는 것을 알고 있었나요?

남 아 맞아요! 댐에 발전소가 있죠, 그렇죠?

여 바로 그거예요. 이것은 깨끗하고 안전해요.

남 태양은 어때요? 그것도 전기를 만들 수 있지 않나요?

여 그래요. 그것은 우리가 "태양 에너지"라고 부르는 거예요.

UNIT VI CONGRATULATIONS!

😊 Check Up

p.37

01 b 02 a

03 A <u>Congratulations on</u> your final exam. You got the best score in the class.

B Well, <u>it was nice of you</u> to help me study, Mrs. Burns.

A Of course. <u>I was glad</u> to help out.

B It was really great of you. <u>I appreciate</u> your time.

Check Up Scripts

01

W Hi, Matt! What have you been doing lately?

M I just graduated from high school.

W That's great! Congratulations on that.

M Thank you. That's so nice of you to say.

W Did you win any awards?

M I was at the top of my class, actually.

여 안녕. Matt! 요즘 뭐 했니?

남 고등학교를 막 졸업했어.

여 잘 됐다! 축하해.

남 고마워. 그렇게 말해주니 정말 고맙다.

여 상은 탔어?

남 사실 우리 반에서 최고 등수였어.

> Vocabulary lately 최근에, 요즘   graduate 졸업하다   award 상   actually 사실

02

M Are you coming to the game tonight?

W Of course! We love to see you play baseball.

M That's very nice of you to say.

W You're playing your old rivals tonight, right?

M Yes, West Park High School. It starts at 7:00.

W We'll get there a half-hour early to get good seats.

M If you come an hour early, you can see the team warm up.

W OK. We'll be there.

남 오늘 밤 경기에 올 거니?

여 당연하지! 우린 네가 야구 경기 하는 걸 보는 게 너무 좋아.

남 그렇게 말해주니 정말 고맙다.

여 오늘 오래된 라이벌과 경기하는 거지?

남 그래. West Park 고등학교야. 7시에 시작해.

여 30분 일찍 가서 좋은 자리를 맡아야겠다.

남 한 시간 일찍 오면 팀이 몸 푸는 걸 볼 수 있어.

여 알겠어. 그때 갈게.

> Vocabulary rival 라이벌, 맞수   seat 좌석   warm up 몸을 풀다

03

A Congratulations on your final exam. You got the best score in the class.

B Well, it was nice of you to help me study, Mrs. Burns.

A Of course. I was glad to help out.

B It was really great of you. I appreciate your time.

A 기말고사에 대해서 축하한다. 네가 우리 반에서 제일 좋은 점수를 받았어.

B 음, 제가 공부하는 것을 도와주셔서 고맙습니다. Burns 선생님.

A 물론이지. 도울 수 있어 기뻤단다.

B 정말 친절하셨어요. 시간을 내 주셔서 감사합니다.

> Vocabulary final exam 기말고사   score 성적, 점수   help out 돕다   appreciate 감사하다

Actual Test

1 ② 2 ② 3 ① 4 ② 5 ③ 6 ⑤ 7 ② 8 ⑤ | p.38

1

W Hi, Greg. <u>How</u> <u>are</u> <u>you</u> feeling today?

M A little better. My leg <u>still</u> <u>hurts</u>, though.

W Yes, I heard <u>you</u> <u>injured</u> <u>it</u> in the basketball game.

M Yeah. Now I have <u>this</u> <u>cast</u>, and I have to walk on <u>crutches</u>.

W I'm so sorry! I hope you feel better soon.

M Thanks. I <u>can't</u> <u>wait</u> <u>to</u> get back on the court!

여 안녕. Greg. 오늘 좀 어떠니?

남 조금 나아졌어. 하지만 아직 다리가 아파.

여 그래. 네가 농구 시합에서 부상을 당했다고 들었어.

남 맞아. 이제 이 깁스를 하고 목발을 짚고 걸어야 해.

여 정말 안됐다! 곧 나아지길 바랄게.

남 고마워. 다시 코트에 돌아가고 싶어 못 견디겠어!

Vocabulary	hurt 아프다 injure 부상을 입다 cast 깁스 crutch 목발

2

M Are you <u>excited</u> <u>about</u> the game tonight?

W I sure am. I can't wait to <u>hit</u> <u>the</u> <u>field</u>!

M Great. As team captain, you have a big responsibility.

W I know, but I'm ready to <u>lead</u> <u>the</u> <u>team</u> to victory.

M Just remember everything I taught you.

W I <u>do</u> <u>appreciate</u> your guidance.

M <u>Don't</u> <u>mention</u> <u>it</u>. Just get out there and win!

남 오늘 밤 경기 때문에 두근거리니?

여 물론이죠. 빨리 경기장에 나가고 싶어요!

남 좋아. 팀의 주장으로서 넌 큰 책임이 있어.

여 알아요. 하지만 전 팀을 승리로 이끌 준비가 되어 있어요.

남 내가 너에게 가르쳐준 모든 걸 기억하기만 하렴.

여 선생님의 지도에 정말 감사해요.

남 천만에. 경기에 나가서 이기거라!

Vocabulary	captain 주장 responsibility 책임 victory 승리 guidance 지도, 조언 reporter 기자

3

M Let me tell you kids an important lesson. Any time you <u>compete</u> <u>against</u> other people, it is important to have good sportsmanship. I used to have a <u>bad</u> <u>attitude</u> about losing at sports. I <u>got</u> <u>really</u> <u>mad</u> <u>at</u> my opponent and sometimes shouted and argued. Then, I realized that it's better to treat others <u>with</u> <u>respect</u>. Instead of getting mad, now I am always nice <u>to</u> <u>my</u> <u>rivals</u>, even if they beat me at something. <u>Instead</u> <u>of</u> <u>making</u> an enemy, I make a new friend.

남 너희들에게 내가 중요한 교훈을 말해줄게. 너희가 다른 사람들과 경쟁할 때면 언제나 좋은 스포츠맨 정신을 갖는 것이 중요하단다. 나는 스포츠에서 지는 것에 대해 안 좋은 태도를 갖고 있었어. 나는 상대편에게 정말 화를 냈고 가끔은 소리를 지르고 말다툼을 하기도 했어. 그러다가 다른 이들을 존중하는 것이 더 낫다는 것을 깨달았지. 이제 나는 화를 내는 대신에 언제나 내 라이벌들에게 좋게 대한단다. 그들이 무언가에서 나를 이길 때도 말이야. 적을 만드는 대신에 나는 새로운 친구를 만든단다.

4

W Great job at the last hockey game, James. It was fun watching you.

M That's really nice of you to say. Do you like hockey?

W It isn't my favorite sport, actually. I prefer baseball.

M But hockey is so exciting! What's not to like about it?

W It's so violent, with all the fighting. I just like quieter games.

여 지난번 하키 시합에서 정말 잘 했어. James. 너를 보는 건 재미있었어.

남 정말 듣기 좋은 말이다. 너 하키 좋아해?

여 사실 내가 제일 좋아하는 스포츠는 아니야. 나는 야구를 더 좋아해.

남 하지만 하키는 너무 신나잖아! 좋아하지 않을 점이 있나?

여 너무 격렬해. 싸움도 많이 나고. 나는 그저 더 조용한 경기들을 좋아해.

5

M Welcome to the 10th annual community picnic! It is so nice of you all to come out for a fun day together. Let me remind you that there is a schedule of events posted near the picnic tables. At 11:00 we will be having a volleyball game. At 12:00, we are serving lunch, followed by live entertainment at 2:00. At 3:00, join the potato sack race! Finally, stay late to watch some fireworks at 7:00!

남 제 10회 연례 주민 소풍에 오신 것을 환영합니다! 여러분 모두가 이렇게 나와서 재미있는 하루를 함께 보내니 정말 좋습니다. 소풍 테이블 근처에 행사 일정표가 붙어 있다는 것을 다시 한 번 알려드립니다. 11시에는 배구 시합을 할 것입니다. 12시에는 점심이 제공될 것이고, 이어서 2시에 라이브로 여흥이 펼쳐지겠습니다. 3시에는 감자 부대 경주에 참여하세요! 마지막으로 7시에 불꽃놀이를 보기 위해 늦게까지 머무르세요!

6

M Congratulations on getting into university, Jane.

W That's nice of you to say. It took a lot of hard work.

M Really? What did you have to do?

W Well, first I had to send applications to many universities.

M And then?

W I had my teachers write letters to recommend me.

M Oh, that's nice of them.

남 대학에 들어간 것 축하해. Jane.

여 그렇게 말해줘서 고마워. 어려운 일이 많았어.

남 정말? 어떤 것을 해야 했는데?

여 음. 우선 많은 대학에 지원서를 보내야 했어.

남 그 다음엔?

여 선생님들께 나를 추천하는 편지를 써달라고 했어.

남 오. 그분들 친절하시네.

W It was. Then, I had to write several essays. Then I had to <u>interview</u> at some of the schools.

M Wow, that does sound like hard work.

여 맞아. 그러고 나서. 에세이를 여러 편 써야 했어. 그 다음에 일부 학교에서 면접을 봐야 했고.

남 와. 정말 어려운 일처럼 들린다.

Vocabulary	university 종합 대학 application 지원서 recommend 추천하다 several 여러 essay 짧은 글
	interview 면접을 보다

M Dear Mr. Kim,

First of all, congratulations <u>on</u> <u>winning</u> your school science fair. It's always great to find <u>a</u> <u>young</u> <u>person</u> so interested in science. We were very impressed <u>with</u> <u>your</u> <u>work</u>. We would like to <u>invite</u> <u>you</u> <u>to</u> <u>compete</u> in this year's International Science Convention in Tokyo. Students from all over the world <u>come</u> <u>to</u> <u>compete</u> in the event. We appreciate your hard work and hope that you <u>will</u> <u>join</u> <u>us</u>.

Sincerely,

Jack Wong

남 친애하는 김 군.

우선. 귀하가 학교 과학 박람회에서 우승한 것을 축하합니다. 젊은 사람이 과학에 그렇게 관심이 많은 것을 발견하는 것은 언제나 기쁜 일입니다. 우리는 귀하의 작품에 깊은 인상을 받았습니다. 우리는 귀하를 도쿄에서 열리는 올해의 국제 과학 대회에 참가자로 초대하고 싶습니다. 전 세계의 학생들이 그 행사에서 경쟁하기 위해 옵니다. 우리는 귀하의 성실한 노력을 높이 평가하고 귀하가 참가하기를 바랍니다.

Jack Wong

Vocabulary	fair 박람회 impress 인상을 주다 invite 초대하다 compete 경쟁하다 international 국제적인
	convention 대회 appreciate 높이 평가하다 join 참가하다 reward 보상하다 inform 알리다

W Hi, Henry. <u>Did</u> <u>you</u> <u>run</u> in the City Marathon last Sunday?

M Yes, I did. I <u>even</u> <u>finished</u> in fourth place!

W <u>Congratulations</u>! How long did it take you?

M About <u>7</u> <u>hours</u>. I began at 7:00 at the North Tower.

W And where did you finish?

M We ran <u>all</u> <u>the</u> <u>way</u> <u>to</u> Freedom Park.

W Great job! I bet you were <u>so</u> <u>tired</u>.

M Yeah, but it was a great experience. Plus, I got a small prize for finishing <u>in</u> <u>fourth</u> <u>place</u>.

여 안녕. Henry. 지난 일요일에 City 마라톤에서 뛰었니?

남 응. 그랬어. 심지어 4등으로 마쳤어!

여 축하해! 얼마나 오래 걸렸니?

남 대략 7시간 정도. 나는 North Tower에서 7시에 출발했어.

여 그리고 어디에서 경주를 끝냈니?

남 우리는 Freedom Park까지 쭉 달렸어.

여 대단하다! 너 정말 피곤했겠다.

남 그래. 하지만 굉장한 경험이었어. 게다가 난 4등으로 마쳐서 작은 상품도 받았어.

Vocabulary	finish 끝마치다. 완주하다 all the way to ~까지 쭉 bet 내기하다 experience 경험 prize 상. 상품

UNIT VII WILL YOU DO ME A FAVOR?

Check Up

p.43

01 a **02** 1.T 2.F 3.F

03 **A** <u>Will you do me a favor</u>, Meg? I need some help studying tonight.

B <u>I'm afraid I can't</u>, because I'm having dinner with my parents this evening.

A That's fine. <u>Can you</u> come over a little later then?

B <u>Sure, I can</u>. How about 8:00?

Check Up Scripts

01

M	Excuse me. Will you do me a favor?	남	실례합니다. 제 부탁 좀 들어주시겠어요?
W	Sure. What is it?	여	그럼요. 무슨 일인가요?
M	I'm trying to find the library.	남	도서관을 찾으려고 하는데요.
W	Oh, that's easy. Go to 1st Street and turn right.	여	오, 그건 쉬워요. 1번가로 가셔서 우회전하세요.
M	OK. What else?	남	네. 그밖에는요?
W	Turn left after the hospital. Then go past the park.	여	병원을 지나서 좌회전하세요. 그리고 나서 공원을 지나 가세요.
M	Is that all?	남	그게 다인가요?
W	Yes, the library is across the street from the bank.	여	네. 도서관은 은행 건너편에 있어요.

> **Vocabulary** do ~ a favor ~의 부탁을 들어주다, ~에게 호의를 베풀다   past ~을 지나   across ~의 건너편에

02

W	Hi, Mark. What are you doing this summer?	여	안녕, Mark. 이번 여름에 뭐 할 거니?
M	Me? I'm traveling abroad.	남	나? 해외 여행을 하려고.
W	That's amazing! Where are you going?	여	그거 굉장하다! 어디로 하는데?
M	I'm spending a week in Paris.	남	파리에서 일주일을 보낼 거야.
W	Would you mind buying me a gift?	여	나한테 선물 하나 사오면 안 될까?
M	Of course! What would you like?	남	당연히 되지! 어떤 걸 받고 싶니?
W	A model of the Eiffel Tower!	여	에펠 탑 모형!
M	Sure, no problem.	남	그래. 문제 없어.

> **Vocabulary** abroad 해외에   spend (시간을) 보내다   mind ~을 꺼리다   model 모형

03

A	Will you do me a favor, Meg? I need some help studying tonight.	A	내 부탁 좀 들어줄래, Meg? 오늘 밤에 공부하는 데 도움이 좀 필요해.
B	I'm afraid I can't, because I'm having dinner with my parents this evening.	B	안 될 것 같아. 오늘 저녁에 부모님이랑 식사를 해.

A That's fine. Can you come over a little later then?

B Sure, I can. How about 8:00?

A 괜찮아. 그러면 좀 늦은 시간에 올 수 있니?

B 그럼. 할 수 있지. 8시 어때?

| Vocabulary | come over 집에 오다 |

Actual Test   1 ④   2 ②   3 ③   4 ③   5 ⑤   6 ⑤   7 ③   8 ③ | p.44

1

W Would you please help me, sir? I can't find my purse.

M Where did you last have it?

W I was at the grocery store. I went there after school.

M And then you came home?

W No, I took the bus to the bank.

M Did you have it on the bus?

W Yes, and I do remember leaving with it.

여 절 좀 도와주시겠어요? 지갑을 찾을 수가 없어요.

남 마지막으로 지갑을 갖고 계셨던 곳이 어디죠?

여 저는 식료품점에 있었어요. 학교가 끝나고 그곳에 갔어요.

남 그 후에 집에 왔나요?

여 아뇨, 버스를 타고 은행에 갔어요.

남 버스에서는 지갑이 있었나요?

여 네, 그리고 내릴 때도 갖고 있었던 걸 분명 기억해요.

| Vocabulary | purse 지갑, 가방   grocery store 식료품점 |

2

W Can I take your order, sir?

M Yes. I'll have a hamburger with cheese, please. Oh, and can you give me fries with that, too?

W Of course. Would you like something to drink?

M A soda would be fine, thank you.

W We have a special on salads today, too.

M That's a bit expensive. I'm afraid it's outside my budget.

W OK. How would you like to pay?

M Here is a 10-dollar bill.

여 주문을 받아도 될까요, 손님?

남 네. 치즈를 곁들인 햄버거 하나 주세요. 오, 그리고 그것과 같이 감자 튀김도 주시겠어요?

여 물론이죠. 음료를 하시겠습니까?

남 탄산음료가 좋겠네요. 고맙습니다.

여 오늘은 샐러드에 스페셜도 있는데요.

남 그건 좀 비싸네요. 제 예산을 벗어나는 것 같아요.

여 알겠습니다. 어떻게 지불하시겠습니까?

남 여기 10달러 지폐가 있습니다.

| Vocabulary | order 주문   fry 감자 튀김   soda 탄산음료   special 특별 요리, 스페셜   expensive 비싼   budget 예산   bill 지폐 |

3

M Dear Sally,

I am having the best summer ever! We

남 Sally에게

나는 최고의 여름을 보내고 있어! 우린 기차를 타고 시골로

boarded a train and <u>took</u> <u>a</u> <u>journey</u> to the countryside. My parents wanted to <u>rest</u> <u>and</u> <u>relax</u>. So we are staying in a cabin on a lake. It is so <u>peaceful</u> <u>and</u> beautiful! But there are fun things to do, too. You asked if I <u>would</u> <u>mind</u> sending you a picture. I don't mind <u>at</u> <u>all</u>!

Thanks,
Michael

여행을 갔어. 부모님은 휴식을 취하고 긴장을 풀고 싶어하셨어. 그래서 우리는 호숫가에 있는 오두막집에서 지내고 있어. 너무 평화롭고 아름다워! 하지만 재미있는 것들도 있어. 내가 사진을 보내줄 수 있는지 물었지. 보내줄 수 있고 말고!

Michael

Vocabulary	board (교통수단을) 타다 journey 여행 countryside 시골 relax 긴장을 풀다 cabin 오두막집
	peaceful 평화로운 mind 꺼리다

W Hello, sir. Can you please help me? I <u>need</u> <u>a</u> <u>ticket</u> to New York.

M When would you like to leave?

W The next <u>possible</u> <u>flight</u>, please.

M And <u>how</u> <u>many</u> <u>passengers</u>?

W Just one: myself. And I have <u>some</u> <u>baggage</u>.

M OK. I can <u>check</u> that for you here.

여 안녕하세요. 저 좀 도와주실 수 있나요? 뉴욕행 표가 필요해요.

남 언제 떠나고 싶으신가요?

여 가능한 가장 빠른 항공편으로 주세요.

남 승객이 몇 분이시죠?

여 저 한 명뿐이에요. 그리고 짐이 좀 있어요.

남 알겠습니다. 짐을 여기서 부쳐드릴게요.

Vocabulary	possible 가능한 flight 항공편 passenger 승객 baggage 짐. 수하물 check (짐을) 부치다

M I <u>need</u> <u>some</u> <u>help</u>, Jan.

W I'd <u>love</u> <u>to</u> help. What is it?

M I have to write about <u>my</u> <u>ideal</u> <u>vacation</u>.

W Hmm. Don't you like <u>the</u> <u>coast</u>?

M I'm <u>not</u> <u>fond</u> of the beach.

W Well, <u>there's</u> <u>also</u> <u>camping</u>. Or going to a city.

M I think I like <u>visiting</u> <u>the</u> <u>mountains</u> the best.

W OK. Well, write about that then.

남 나 도움이 좀 필요해. Jan.

여 돕고 싶어. 무슨 일인데?

남 내 이상적인 휴가에 대해 써야 해.

여 흠. 해안 지방을 좋아하지 않니?

남 나는 바닷가를 별로 안 좋아해.

여 음. 캠핑도 있어. 아니면 도시를 방문하는 것도 있고.

남 나는 산에 가는 걸 제일 좋아하는 것 같아.

여 알겠어. 음. 그럼 그것에 대해 써봐.

Vocabulary	ideal 이상적인 vacation 휴가 coast 해안 (지방)

M Every year, the Spanish students take a special trip. We study Spanish among <u>native</u> <u>speakers</u>. Last year, we visited Seville. But we need to <u>raise</u> <u>some</u> <u>money</u> for this year's trip. Last year we spent $10,000. We got 30% of

남 해마다 스페인어 반 학생들은 특별한 여행을 떠납니다. 우리는 모국어 사용자들 사이에서 스페인어를 공부합니다. 작년에 우리는 세빌랴를 방문했습니다. 하지만 우리는 올해의 여행을 위해 모금을 해야 합니다. 작년에 우리는 1만 달러를 썼습니다. 우리는 과자를 팔아서 30%의 자금을 얻었

our money from selling cookies. Another 20% came from donations from the community. 20% was given to us by the school. 15% came from parents, and the last 15% came from us club members.

습니다. 또 다른 20%는 지역사회의 기부금에서 얻었습니다. 20%가 학교에서 제공되었고 15%가 학부모로부터 왔습니다. 그리고 마지막 15%는 클럽 회원들인 우리들로부터 왔습니다.

7

W Are you looking for the perfect romantic vacation? Look no further than Gulf Island. Relax on our beautiful beaches. Watch the dolphins play just off the coast. Eat wonderful fresh seafood. Gulf Island has everything you are looking for and more! And no matter where you live, Gulf Island is never too far away. A short domestic flight is all it takes to get here. So confirm your reservation at one of our resorts today!

여 완벽한 낭만적인 휴가를 찾고 계신가요? Gulf 섬 말고 다른 곳을 찾지 마세요. 우리의 아름다운 해변에서 휴식을 취하세요. 해안 바로 근처에서 돌고래들이 노는 것을 지켜보세요. 훌륭한 신선한 해산물을 드세요. Gulf 섬은 당신이 찾는 모든 것과 그 이상을 갖고 있습니다! 그리고 당신이 어디에 사시더라도 Gulf 섬은 그리 멀지 않습니다. 짧은 국내 항공편을 이용하시기만 하면 이곳에 오실 수 있습니다. 그러니 오늘 우리 리조트 중 한 곳에 예약을 확정하세요!

8

① M We could really use a vacation this summer.
W I agree. How about we talk to a travel agent?
② W I can't believe we got lost in the city.
M Good thing we were able to locate a police officer to help.
③ M Can you please help me book a flight?
W I'm afraid I can't accept a credit card.
④ W Hi. I'd like to confirm my reservation.
M No problem. What is your last name?
⑤ M Do you think we should take the bus?
W I don't think so. It's only a short walk.

① 남 우리는 이번 여름에 정말로 휴가를 쓸 수 있을 거야.
여 나도 그렇게 생각해. 여행사 직원에게 상담해 보는 게 어떨까?
② 여 우리가 도시에서 길을 잃었다니 믿기지 않아.
남 다행인 것은 도움을 줄 경찰관을 찾을 수 있었다는 거야.
③ 남 항공권 예약하는 것 좀 도와주실래요?
여 죄송하지만 신용 카드는 받을 수 없습니다.
④ 여 안녕하세요. 제 예약 내역을 확인하고 싶습니다.
남 문제 없습니다. 성이 어떻게 되십니까?
⑤ 남 우리가 그 버스를 타야 한다고 생각해?
여 그렇게 생각하지 않아. 짧게 걸어갈 수 있는 거리야.

UNIT VIII WHY DO YOU THINK SO?

Check Up

p.49

01 b

02

	Judge	Professor
Respected	✓	
Very smart		✓
Important	✓	

03 **A** <u>Can you tell me why</u> you decided to become an author?

B Well, I love telling stories. <u>That's why</u> I write books.

A I think it's hard to become a writer nowadays.

B <u>What makes you say</u> that?

A <u>Because</u> people are buying and reading fewer books these days.

Check Up Scripts

01

a. A student is speaking to the class.

b. A professor is teaching a class.

c. A teacher is talking to a student.

a. 한 학생이 반 학생들에게 말을 하고 있다.

b. 한 교수가 수업을 하고 있다.

c. 한 선생님이 한 학생에게 이야기를 하고 있다.

> **Vocabulary** professor 교수

02

M I think being a judge would be a great career.

W Why do you think so?

M It's a very important job. And judges are very respected.

W I would do better as a professor, I think.

M What makes you say that?

W Professors are really smart, and so am I.

남 나는 판사가 되는 것이 아주 좋은 직업일 것 같아.

여 왜 그렇게 생각하니?

남 아주 중요한 직업이잖아. 그리고 판사들은 크게 존경받아.

여 나는 교수를 하면 더 잘 할 것 같아.

남 왜 그렇게 말하니?

여 교수들은 정말 똑똑하잖아. 그리고 나도 그렇고.

> **Vocabulary** judge 판사　career 직업　respected 존경받는　smart 똑똑한

03

A Can you tell me why you decided to become an author?

B Well, I love telling stories. That's why I write books.

A I think it's hard to become a writer nowadays.

B What makes you say that?

A 왜 작가가 되기로 결심하셨는지 말씀해주시겠어요?

B 음. 저는 이야기를 하는 것을 정말 좋아해요. 그래서 책을 쓰는 것이죠.

A 요즘은 작가가 되는 것이 어려운 거 같아요.

B 왜 그렇게 말씀하시죠?

A Because people are buying and reading fewer books these days.

A 왜냐하면 요즘은 사람들이 점점 더 책을 적게 사 읽으니까요.

Actual Test   1 ④   2 ⑤   3 ①   4 ③   5 ④   6 ①   7 ②   8 ④ | p.50

W It's so hard to choose a good career!

M Why do you say so, Miko?

W There are so many! How will I ever choose?

M Think about something you are good at doing.

W Hm. I like to organize things, like my bedroom closet.

M Maybe you would enjoy being a secretary.

W Why do you think so?

M They spend all day organizing files, meetings, phone calls, and more.

여 좋은 직업을 고르기가 너무 어려워!

남 왜 그렇게 말해, Miko?

여 너무 많은 직업이 있어! 내가 어떻게 고르겠어?

남 네가 잘 하는 것에 대해 생각해봐.

여 흠. 나는 정리하는 걸 좋아해. 이를 테면 내 침실 벽장 같은 것 말이야.

남 넌 어쩌면 비서가 되는 걸 좋아할 수 있겠다.

여 왜 그렇게 생각하니?

남 그들은 하루 종일 파일, 회의, 전화, 그밖에 다른 것들을 정리하잖아.

M Ladies and gentlemen, this city needs great leadership. You deserve a mayor that will listen to your ideas and your complaints. Someone who will listen, and will do something about it. And ladies and gentlemen, I am that man. Vote for me this Tuesday in the election. Elect me mayor, and we can change this city for the better!

남 신사 숙녀 여러분, 이 도시는 위대한 지도력을 필요로 합니다. 여러분은 여러분의 생각과 불만에 귀 기울일 시장을 가질 권리가 있습니다. 들어줄 누군가, 그리고 그것에 대해 무엇인가를 할 누군가 말입니다. 그리고, 신사 숙녀 여러분, 제가 그 사람입니다. 이번 화요일에 선거에서 저에게 투표해 주십시오. 저를 시장으로 당선시켜 주십시오. 그러면 우리는 이 도시를 더 나은 곳으로 변화시킬 수 있습니다!

W People think it's easy to be a professional movie critic. I ask people, "What makes you say so?" They think we just sit around watching movies all the time. In reality, it's quite difficult to become a professional critic. You have to

여 사람들은 전문 영화 평론가가 되는 것이 쉽다고 생각합니다. 저는 사람들에게 "왜 그렇게 말하십니까?"라고 묻습니다. 그들은 우리가 그저 빈둥거리고 앉아서 늘 영화나 본다고 생각합니다. 실제로는 전문적인 평론가가 되는 것은 매우 어렵습니다. 정식 기자로 일을 시작해야 하고, 뉴스 기사를

start as a regular journalist, writing news stories. That's why I tell people to study journalism if they want to one day become a critic.

써야 합니다. 그래서 제가 사람들에게 언젠가 평론가가 되고 싶다면 저널리즘을 공부하라고 말하는 것입니다.

Vocabulary	professional 전문적인, 프로의 critic 평론가, 비평가 sit around 빈둥거리다 in reality 실제로는, 현실에서는
	regular 정식의, 정규의 journalist 기자, 언론인 journalism 저널리즘

4

W Hey, Mark. What's wrong?

M I'm going to the school dance tonight.

W But that's going to be fun, right?

M Well, I went to the barber to get my hair cut, and he totally ruined it. Look at this! It looks awful!

W Why do you say that?

M It's too short and it's really messy, that's why!

W Well, I don't think a bad haircut will ruin your night.

M I hope you're right! I'm definitely never going back to that barber.

여 야, Mark. 무슨 일 있어?

남 오늘 밤에 학교 댄스 파티에 가.

여 하지만 그건 재미있을 거잖아. 응?

남 음. 머리를 자르러 이발소에 갔는데 이발사가 머리를 완전히 망쳐놨어. 이걸 좀 봐! 끔찍해 보여!

여 왜 그렇게 말하니?

남 너무 짧고 정말 지저분해. 그래서야!

여 음, 머리 모양이 나쁘다고 해서 오늘 밤을 망치게 될 것 같지는 않은데.

남 네 말이 맞으면 좋겠다! 난 절대 그 이발사에게 다시 가지 않을 거야.

Vocabulary	school dance 학교 댄스 파티 barber 이발사 get a haircut 머리를 자르다 totally 완전히 ruin 망치다
	awful 끔찍한, 형편없는 messy 지저분한 nervous 초조한, 긴장된

5

[The telephone rings.]

W John, today is the best day ever!

M What makes you say so, Beth?

W My father is finally coming home today! He's a soldier who's been overseas. We're having a party, but there's a lot to do first.

M When do you pick up your father at the airport?

W At 2:00. But first thing, I have to order a cake.

M You should buy him some flowers, I think.

W Yes. I'll do that next, at the florist. Then I'll pick up steak for dinner.

M Sounds great. We're still meeting for lunch at noon, right?

W Of course! I can't wait.

[전화벨 소리]

여 John, 오늘은 최고의 날이야!

남 왜 그렇게 말하는 거야, Beth?

여 우리 아빠가 오늘 드디어 집에 오셔! 아빠는 군인인데 해외에 나가 계셨거든. 우린 파티를 할 거야. 그런데 먼저 해야 할 일이 많아.

남 공항에 아버지를 모시러 언제 갈 거야?

여 2시에. 하지만 제일 먼저, 케이크를 주문해야 해.

남 꽃을 좀 사드려야 할 것 같은데.

여 그래. 그 다음에 꽃가게에 가서 꽃을 살 거야. 그리고 나서 저녁에 먹을 스테이크를 찾아올 거야.

남 좋은 계획이네. 우린 그래도 정오에 만나서 점심 먹는 거지?

여 물론이지! 너무 기다려져.

M I have always been very compassionate, and I love to <u>listen</u> to people's problems. Sometimes, I can even help them find peace. <u>That's</u> <u>why</u> I love what I do. I had to study a lot to become what I am today. Mostly, I <u>read</u> <u>the</u> Bible a lot. But all the hard work was worth it. Now I <u>get</u> <u>to</u> <u>serve</u> my community and my God every day.

남 저는 언제나 동정심이 아주 많았고 사람들의 문제에 귀기울이는 것을 좋아합니다. 때때로 저는 그들이 마음의 평안을 얻도록 도울 수 있습니다. 그래서 저는 제가 하는 일을 사랑합니다. 저는 오늘날의 제가 되기 위해 많이 공부해야 했습니다. 주로 저는 성경을 많이 읽었습니다. 하지만 그 모든 힘든 일들은 가치가 있었습니다. 이제 저는 날마다 제 지역 주민들과 제가 믿는 신을 섬깁니다.

① **M** I am a <u>professor</u> <u>of</u> biology at the university.

   W Wow. You must be an <u>expert</u> <u>on</u> <u>the</u> <u>subject</u>.

② **W** We should <u>call</u> <u>the</u> <u>police</u> about all the noise outside.

   M No, I think firemen have <u>the</u> <u>bravest</u> job.

③ **M** Why do you think people like <u>horror</u> <u>movies</u>?

   W Some people just like <u>to</u> <u>be</u> <u>scared</u> sometimes.

④ **W** I don't understand the <u>directions</u> <u>for</u> <u>the</u> <u>assignment</u>.

   M <u>Don't</u> <u>worry</u>. I can explain it to you later.

⑤ **M** Traffic is really bad <u>on</u> <u>the</u> <u>freeway</u> today.

   W <u>That's</u> <u>why</u> I am taking the subway instead.

① 남 저는 대학에서 생물학을 가르치는 교수입니다.

   여 와. 그 학문 분야의 전문가이시겠네요.

② 여 밖에서 나는 저 모든 소음에 대해 경찰에 신고해야 겠어.

   남 아니야. 나는 소방관들이 가장 용감한 일을 한다고 생각해.

③ 남 너는 사람들이 왜 공포 영화를 좋아한다고 생각하니?

   여 어떤 사람들은 그냥 가끔씩 겁에 질리는 걸 좋아해.

④ 여 나는 이 과제에 대한 지시 사항을 이해 못하겠어.

   남 걱정 마. 내가 나중에 설명해 줄게.

⑤ 남 오늘 고속도로에 차가 너무 막히네.

   여 그래서 내가 그 대신 지하철을 타는 거야.

M When I grow up, I'm going to <u>be</u> <u>an</u> <u>astronaut</u>.

W <u>Can</u> <u>you</u> <u>tell</u> <u>me</u> <u>why</u> you want to do that?

M Astronauts get to travel in space. They are so brave.

남 나는 나중에 크면 우주 비행사가 될 거야.

여 왜 그러고 싶은지 말해줄 수 있니?

남 우주 비행사들은 우주를 여행할 수 있잖아. 그들은 정말 용감해.

W	It's difficult to become an astronaut.	여	우주 비행사가 되는 건 힘들어.
M	Yes, it is. That is why I am already making plans.	남	그래. 힘들지. 그래서 나는 벌써 계획을 세우고 있어.
W	It's also somewhat dangerous.	여	또 약간 위험하기도 해.
M	That doesn't matter. I have the courage to face danger.	남	그건 상관 없어. 나는 위험에 맞설 용기가 있어.
W	Well, best of luck to you!	여	음, 행운을 빈다!

UNIT IX PLEASE LET ME TRY.

Check Up

p.55

01 b 02 1.F 2.T 3.F

03 **A** Hello, I want to complain about a bad product. I bought this device at your store yesterday, but it doesn't work.

B Did you drop the product or break it in any way?

A Of course not! I can't understand why you would ask me that.

B My apologies, but we have to ask. Let's try this, OK? We will exchange the product for another of the same type.

Check Up Scripts

01

a.	W	I want to complain about the computer I bought here.	a.	여	전 여기서 산 컴퓨터에 대해 불만을 말하고 싶어요.
	M	Of course. What seems to be the problem?		남	알겠습니다. 문제가 무엇인지요?
b.	W	Is this the best television that you have?	b.	여	이게 갖고 계신 가장 좋은 텔레비전인가요?
	M	In my opinion, it's the top of the line.		남	제 생각에는 최고의 제품입니다.
c.	W	I'd like to buy a new stereo. Can you help me?	c.	여	전 새 스테레오를 사고 싶어요. 도와주시겠어요?
	M	Of course. Why don't I show you this one?		남	그럼요. 이 제품을 보여드리면 어떨까요?

02

W	Hi. I'm shopping for a new television.	여	안녕하세요. 새 텔레비전을 사려고 하는데요.
M	What features would you like?	남	어떤 기능을 원하시나요?

W Um, definitely a big screen and loud speakers.

M OK. Do you want a flat screen TV?

W Yes, that would be best.

M Let's try this one. It's the newest model.

여 음. 큰 화면과 큰 스피커는 꼭 있어야죠.

남 알겠습니다. 평면 TV를 원하시나요?

여 네. 그게 제일 좋겠네요.

남 이 제품을 한번 써보세요. 최신 모델입니다.

> Vocabulary feature 기능 definitely 꼭. 반드시 try 한번 써보다

03

A Hello, I want to complain about a bad product. I bought this device at your store yesterday, but it doesn't work.

B Did you drop the product or break it in any way?

A Of course not! I can't understand why you would ask me that.

B My apologies, but we have to ask. Let's try this, OK? We will exchange the product for another of the same type.

A 안녕하세요. 불량품에 대해 불만을 말하고 싶습니다. 어제 댁의 가게에서 이 장치를 구입했는데 작동을 안 해요.

B 혹시 제품을 떨어뜨리거나 어떤 식으로든 손상시키셨나요?

A 당연히 아니죠! 왜 그런 걸 물으시는지 이해가 안 되네요.

B 죄송합니다만 여쭤봐야 합니다. 이렇게 해보죠. 어떠세요? 저희가 제품을 같은 종류의 새 제품으로 교환해 드리겠습니다.

> Vocabulary complain 불평하다 device 장치 drop 떨어뜨리다 break 망가뜨리다 apology 사과 exchange 교환하다

Actual Test
1 ③ 2 ④ 3 ② 4 ③ 5 ② 6 ③ 7 ② 8 ⑤ | p.56

W I'm traveling to California on Tuesday.

M I hope you have fun. Are you traveling nonstop?

W No, there is a short stopover. I can't understand why.

M Well, it's a long way. Maybe it needs to land and get more fuel.

W I guess you're right. Something that big probably needs a lot of fuel.

M Yeah. Don't worry about it. I'm sure it won't take long.

여 나는 화요일에 캘리포니아로 여행을 떠나.

남 재미있게 지내면 좋겠다. 직항으로 가니?

여 아니야. 잠깐 동안 경유가 있어. 이유는 모르겠지만.

남 음. 먼 길이잖아. 어쩌면 착륙해서 연료를 더 채워야 할지도 몰라.

여 네 말이 맞을 것 같다. 그렇게 커다란 물건은 아마 많은 연료를 필요로 하겠지.

남 그래. 그건 걱정하지 마. 오래 걸리지는 않을 거야.

> Vocabulary nonstop 직항으로, 쉬지 않고 stopover 경유 land 착륙하다 fuel 연료

W I bought this MP3 player, but it doesn't work right.

여 이 MP3 플레이어를 샀는데 잘 작동하지 않네.

M	Have you tried reading the directions?	남	설명서 읽어봤어?
W	Yes, but they are kind of hard to understand.	여	응. 그런데 이해하기가 좀 어려워.
M	What is the problem exactly?	남	문제가 정확히 뭔데?
W	I can't copy music from my computer.	여	음악을 컴퓨터로부터 못 옮기겠어.
M	Please let me try. I have my own MP3 player at home. Oh, I see the problem. It has a small capacity.	남	내가 한번 해볼게. 집에 내 MP3 플레이어가 있거든. 오, 문제가 뭔지 알겠어. 용량이 작아.
W	What do you mean?	여	무슨 말이야?
M	It can hold up to 500 songs, but no more.	남	500곡까지 담을 수 있는데 그 이상은 안 돼.

> **Vocabulary** direction 설명서, 지시 사항 exactly 정확히 copy 복사하다 capacity 용량 hold 담다

W	Cleaning house can be a real chore sometimes, especially when you have to sweep and vacuum all the floors. Now, there's a better way to keep your house sparkling clean. It's the Zoom Vac! The Zoom Vac is completely automatic. All you have to do is turn it on! It rolls around your house sucking dirt and dust right off your floor. So if you're looking for an easier way to clean your floors, try this today!	여	집을 청소하는 것은 때때로 정말 힘든 일이 될 수 있습니다. 특히 바닥을 쓸고 진공청소기로 청소해야 할 때 그렇죠. 이제, 여러분의 집을 반짝반짝 빛나도록 깨끗하게 유지할 더 좋은 방법이 생겼습니다. 바로 Zoom Vac입니다! Zoom Vac은 전자동입니다. 여러분이 해야 하는 것은 전원을 켜는 것뿐입니다! 그것은 여러분의 집안을 돌아다니며 오물과 먼지를 바닥에서 바로 빨아들입니다. 그러니 바닥을 청소하는 더 쉬운 방법을 찾고 있다면 이 제품을 오늘 써보세요!

> **Vocabulary** chore 집안일 sweep 쓸다 vacuum 진공청소기로 청소하다 sparkling 반짝이는 automatic 자동의 turn on ~을 켜다 suck 빨아들이다 dirt 더러운 것 dust 먼지

	[The telephone rings.]		[전화벨 소리]
M	Excuse me, I bought a video game from you recently, but it doesn't work.	남	실례합니다. 최근에 귀사에서 비디오 게임을 샀는데 작동하지 않습니다.
W	What is the name of the game, sir?	여	게임의 이름이 무엇인가요, 고객님?
M	It's called "Aircraft Extreme."	남	'Aircraft Extreme'입니다.
W	OK. Let's try this. How about you return it for a refund?	여	알겠습니다. 이렇게 해보죠. 반품하셔서 환불을 받으시는 게 어떻겠습니까?
M	That's fine. I bought it online, though.	남	좋습니다. 하지만 온라인으로 구입했는데요.
W	Just mail it back to us, and we will mail you a refund check.	여	그냥 저희에게 우편으로 돌려보내 주시면 저희가 환불 수표를 부쳐드리겠습니다.
M	OK. What about shipping costs?	남	알겠습니다. 배송비는요?
W	We can't refund those, sir. I'm sorry.	여	배송비는 환불해 드리지 않습니다, 고객님. 죄송합니다.
M	I can't understand why not. I paid $75 for the game and shipping.	남	왜 안 되는지 이해를 못 하겠네요. 게임과 배송비로 75달러를 냈다구요.

W It's store policy. We can't refund the $15 shipping charge.

여 판매 정책입니다. 배송비 15달러는 환불해 드릴 수 없습니다.

5

W I can't understand why gasoline has to be so expensive!

여 휘발유가 왜 그렇게 비싸야 하는지 이해 못하겠어!

M I know. It costs me $10 a day just to get to work by car these days.

남 알아. 요즘은 차로 출근하려면 하루에 10달러가 들어.

W What types of transportation do you use now instead?

여 그 대신 지금 어떤 교통수단을 이용하니?

M Well, the bus is much cheaper. I can commute for $4.

남 음. 버스는 훨씬 싸. 4달러에 통근할 수 있어.

W How about the subway?

여 지하철은 어때?

M It's a bit more. $6 a day is enough to ride the subway, though.

남 조금 더 들어. 하지만 지하철을 타는 데 하루에 6달러면 충분해.

W Have you tried taxis?

여 택시는 시도해 봤니?

M It's too far. It would cost at least $30 a day.

남 거리가 너무 멀어. 하루에 적어도 30달러는 들 거야.

W Hmm. What about a bike?

여 흠. 자전거는 어때?

M I guess that would cost almost nothing.

남 그건 거의 돈이 안 들겠네.

6

M Today, we had a big test in class. I studied a little bit, but not too much. After all, science is my favorite class. I love reading about science all the time. But when I got my test back, I made a very bad grade. I didn't understand how it could happen. I thought I was really good at it. But I guess I'll need to work a little harder next time if I want to make the grade. I learned an important lesson about being prepared.

남 오늘 우리는 수업시간에 중요한 시험을 봤다. 나는 약간 공부를 했지만 많이 하지는 않았다. 어쨌거나 과학은 내가 제일 좋아하는 수업이니까. 나는 언제나 과학에 대해 읽는 것을 정말 좋아한다. 하지만 내가 시험지를 되돌려 받았을 때 나는 아주 좋지 않은 성적을 받았다. 나는 어떻게 그런 일이 일어날 수 있었는지 이해할 수 없었다. 나는 내가 그것[과학]을 정말 잘 한다고 생각했던 것이다. 하지만 다음 번에 내가 어느 정도 좋은 성적을 받고 싶으면 좀 더 열심히 노력해야 할 것 같다. 나는 준비하는 것에 대한 중요한 교훈을 얻었다.

7

W This is Principal Walton speaking. I only want to remind students that final exams will be

여 Walton 교장입니다. 다음 주에 모든 수업에서 기말고사가 있다는 것을 학생들에게 다시 한 번 알려드립니다. 이

held next week in all classes. Without passing these tests, you will not be able to advance to the next grade level. So it is very important that you are ready to perform well on test day. I suggest you try this: get a full night's sleep and eat a healthy breakfast. That's a good way to make sure your mind is sharp.

시험들을 통과하지 못하면 다음 학년으로 진급할 수 없을 것입니다. 그러니 시험 당일에 실력을 발휘할 준비가 되어 있는 것이 매우 중요합니다. 여러분이 이렇게 하도록 권합니다. 밤에 충분히 잘 자고 건강에 좋은 아침식사를 먹는 것입니다. 그것은 여러분의 정신이 말똥말똥하도록 확실히 하는 좋은 방법입니다.

| Vocabulary | principal 교장   remind 일깨우다, 상기시키다   final exam 기말고사   pass 통과하다   advance 진급하다 |
| | grade 학년   perform 수행하다   suggest 제안하다, 권하다   healthy 건강에 좋은   on time 제시간에 |

M I really want to build robots one day. Aren't they cool?

W Yes, robots are interesting. They're so much smarter these days.

M I know. It's called artificial intelligence. They think like people.

W That sounds kind of creepy to me, actually.

M I can't understand why you would think that.

W Well, what if they become dangerous to humans?

M Oh, they're perfectly safe. They only do what they're told.

W That's true. But they might still hurt people on accident.

Question What statement best describes the situation?

① The man and woman agree that robots are safe.
② The woman wants to build robots one day.
③ The man and woman are having an argument.
④ The man is against creating smart robots.
⑤ The man and woman disagree about robots.

남 나는 언젠가 정말 로봇을 만들고 싶어. 로봇은 멋지지 않니?

여 그래. 로봇은 흥미롭지. 요즘 로봇들은 훨씬 똑똑해졌어.

남 알아. 인공지능이라고 하지. 그것들은 인간처럼 생각해.

여 사실 그건 나에게는 좀 징그럽게 들려.

남 왜 네가 그렇게 생각하는지 이해할 수 없는데.

여 음. 그것들이 인간에게 위험해지면 어떻게 해?

남 오. 그것들은 완전히 안전해. 그것들은 명령받은 대로 행동할 뿐이야.

여 그건 그래. 하지만 그래도 사고로 사람을 다치게 할지도 몰라.

질문 상황을 가장 잘 설명하는 문장은 무엇인가?

① 남자와 여자는 로봇이 안전하다는 것에 동의한다.

② 여자는 언젠가 로봇을 만들고 싶어 한다.
③ 남자와 여자는 말다툼을 하고 있다.

④ 남자는 똑똑한 로봇을 만드는 것에 반대한다.

⑤ 남자와 여자는 로봇에 대해 의견이 다르다.

| Vocabulary | artificial 인공의   intelligence 지능   creepy 징그러운   human 인간   hurt 다치게 하다   on accident 사고로, 우연히 |
| | argument 말다툼, 언쟁   create 만들다 |

UNIT X I HOPE TO VISIT PARIS ONE DAY.

Check Up

p.61

01 a **02** c

03 A Trish, I'm having a party on Saturday. I hope that you can come.

   B Oh, I wish I could, but I can't. I'm planning to visit my family Saturday.

   A OK. Well, have fun. I hope to see you at the next party.

   B Of course!

Check Up Scripts

01

W What do you plan to do in the mountains, Mike?

M Well, I do enjoy mountain climbing.

W That sounds really challenging to me.

M You're right. I'll probably just go hiking this time.

W That's my favorite thing to do.

M Me too. One day, though, I hope to learn mountain biking.

여 산에서 뭘 하려고 계획 중이니, Mike?

남 음. 난 등산을 정말 좋아해.

여 그건 나한텐 너무 어려운 것처럼 들린다.

남 네 말이 맞아. 이번엔 그냥 하이킹이나 할까 봐.

여 그게 내가 제일 좋아하는 거야.

남 나도야. 하지만 언젠가는 산악 자전거를 배우고 싶어.

Vocabulary	mountain climbing 등산, 등반 challenging 어려운, 도전적인 hiking 하이킹, 가벼운 등산 mountain biking 산악 자전거

02

W What are you doing after school today?

M I'm planning to go to the mall with friends.

W That's always fun. Can I come too?

M I'm not sure if we're going yet. But it is likely.

W Great. Let me know what you decide.

여 오늘 학교 끝나고 뭐 할 거야?

남 친구들이랑 쇼핑몰에 갈까 생각 중이야.

여 그건 언제나 재미있지. 나도 가도 돼?

남 우리가 갈 건지 아직 확실히 모르겠어. 하지만 갈 것 같아.

여 좋아. 결정하면 알려줘.

Vocabulary	mall 쇼핑몰 yet 아직 likely 가능성이 많은 decide 결정하다

03

A Trish, I'm having a party on Saturday. I hope that you can come.

B Oh, I wish I could, but I can't. I'm planning to visit my family Saturday.

A OK. Well, have fun. I hope to see you at the next party.

B Of course!

A Trish. 내가 토요일에 파티를 하는데 네가 올 수 있으면 좋겠어.

B 오, 갈 수 있었으면 좋겠는데 못 가. 토요일에 가족을 방문할 생각이거든.

A 그렇구나. 음. 재미있게 지내다 와. 다음 번 파티에서 보면 좋겠다.

B 물론이지!

Vocabulary	have fun 즐겁게 지내다

W Did you know that stop signs are different all over the world?

M Yeah, I know. I love to travel, so I hope to see them all one day.

W Here in America they are mostly red, with eight sides.

M True. I hear that in Kuwait they also have eight sides, but are mostly white.

W I traveled to Japan once and saw an upside-down, red triangle.

M Interesting. Some old stop signs in Europe also have triangles, but with a circle.

여 정지 표지판이 세계적으로 다르다는 거 알았어?

남 응. 알고 있어. 난 여행하는 걸 정말 좋아해서 언젠가 그것들을 모두 보고 싶어.

여 여기 미국에서는 정지 표지판이 대부분 빨간색이고 팔각형이야.

남 그래. 쿠웨이트에서도 팔각형인데 대부분 흰색이라고 하더라.

여 난 전에 한번 일본 여행을 갔었는데 거꾸로 된 빨간 삼각형을 봤어.

남 재미있네. 유럽의 어떤 오래된 정지 표지판에도 삼각형이 있는데 원이 같이 있어.

Vocabulary	stop sign 정지 표지판 mostly 대부분 side 면 upside-down 거꾸로 뒤집힌 once 한번은 triangle 삼각형 circle 원

M Are you excited about tomorrow's field trip?

W I can hardly wait! I love the science museum.

M Me too, but I have been there many times.

W So I guess it's kind of boring for you now.

M Not always. Of course, I do hope to see something new.

W I'm sure you will. I think they made some recent updates.

남 내일 현장 학습 때문에 신나니?

여 못 기다리겠어! 난 과학 박물관이 너무 좋아.

남 나도야. 하지만 난 그곳에 여러 번 가봤어.

여 그럼 이제 너에게는 좀 지루하겠구나.

남 항상 그렇지는 않아. 물론 새로운 것을 좀 보고 싶어.

여 분명히 그럴 거야. 새로 업데이트를 했을 것 같아.

Vocabulary	field trip 현장 학습 hardly 거의 ~ 않다 museum 박물관 boring 지루한 recent 최근의 update 업데이트

W When I was a little girl, I loved watching airplanes fly overhead. I wanted to be on them going someplace exciting and new. At home, everything is so ordinary! Now that I'm older, I have the opportunity to travel a little bit, and I am so excited. Mostly, I want to tour Western Europe and see all the beautiful cities. I plan to do that when I graduate.

여 제가 어린 소녀였을 때, 저는 비행기가 머리 위로 날아가는 것을 보는 걸 정말 좋아했어요. 저는 그것을 타고 어딘가 신나고 새로운 곳으로 가고 싶었어요. 집에서는 모든 것이 너무나 평범해요! 제가 이제 나이가 드니까 여행을 다닐 기회가 좀 생겨서 너무 신나요. 저는 주로 서유럽을 여행하면서 그 모든 아름다운 도시들을 보고 싶어요. 저는 졸업하면 그걸 하려고 계획 중이에요.

4

W Hi, Bill. I see you're <u>shopping</u> <u>for</u> groceries.	**여** 안녕. Bill. 보니까 너 식료품 사러 왔구나.
M Yes. I'm having a barbecue this weekend.	**남** 응. 이번 주말에 바비큐를 해.
W That <u>sounds</u> <u>like</u> <u>fun</u>. Is it a party?	**여** 재미있겠다. 파티야?
M Yes. In fact, it's my friend Toby's birthday.	**남** 응. 사실은 내 친구 Toby의 생일이야.
W <u>How</u> <u>exciting</u>. I hope you have a great time.	**여** 정말 재미있겠네. 즐거운 시간을 보내길 바라.
M Oh, <u>we</u> <u>plan</u> <u>to</u>. You're welcome to come, if you like.	**남** 오. 그러려고 해. 오고 싶다면 너도 환영이야.
W Sure. I <u>have</u> <u>no</u> <u>plans</u> this weekend.	**여** 좋아. 난 이번 주말에 계획이 없어.
M Great. <u>Bring</u> <u>your</u> <u>daughter</u>, too. There will be lots of kids there.	**남** 잘 됐네. 네 딸도 데려와. 애들이 많이 올 거야.
W I'll do that. See you soon, Bill.	**여** 그럴게. 곧 봐. Bill.

5

M Here's some <u>interesting</u> <u>news</u> for you star watchers out there. This weekend there will be many <u>falling</u> <u>stars</u> in the northern sky. It should happen around 2:00 <u>in</u> <u>the</u> <u>morning</u>. Something like this <u>doesn't</u> <u>happen</u> <u>often</u>, so bring your telescope and enjoy it while you can. Also, there will be an event at <u>Hill</u> <u>Park</u> that night to celebrate. <u>I'm</u> <u>going</u> <u>to</u> be there, and I encourage you to come as well.	**남** 별을 관측하는 여러분들께 조금 흥미로운 소식이 있습니다. 이번 주말에 북쪽 창공에서 유성우가 있을 것입니다. 그것은 새벽 2시경에 일어날 것입니다. 이런 일은 자주 일어나지 않으니, 망원경을 가지고 가서 즐기실 수 있을 때 즐기세요. 또한 그날 밤에 기념하기 위해서 Hill Park에서 행사가 있을 것입니다. 저도 거기에 참석하려고 하니 여러분도 와주시면 좋겠습니다.

6

M Excuse me, ma'am? <u>I</u> <u>think</u> <u>I'm</u> <u>lost</u>.	**남** 실례합니다. 부인? 제가 길을 잃은 것 같아요.
W Where do you want to go?	**여** 어디로 가고 싶으세요?
M I need to get to the mall. I <u>plan</u> <u>to</u> <u>meet</u> my family there.	**남** 쇼핑몰에 가야 합니다. 거기서 가족을 만나려고요.
W <u>Go</u> <u>to</u> <u>the</u> <u>end</u> of Pine Street and turn left.	**여** Pine Street로 가서 좌회전하세요.
M OK.	**남** 네.
W At the school, <u>turn</u> <u>right</u> on Elm Street.	**여** 학교에서 Elm Street로 우회전하세요.
M And that's where the mall is?	**남** 그곳이 쇼핑몰이 있는 곳인가요?
W Yes. You will see it <u>on</u> <u>the</u> <u>right</u>, past Market Street.	**여** 네. Market Street을 지나서 오른쪽으로 보일 거예요.
M Thank you for <u>taking</u> <u>a</u> <u>moment</u> to help!	**남** 시간을 내어 도와주셔서 감사합니다!

W In other news, the famous Grant Diamond has been stolen from its place in the city museum. This incident occurred sometime late last night. Police have no idea how the robbers got into the museum without being caught. The diamond is the largest of its kind, and is very, very valuable. A policeman on the scene said they are thinking of bringing in experts to solve the case.

여 다른 소식입니다. 유명한 Grant Diamond가 시립 박물관에 보관된 자리에서 도둑맞았습니다. 이 사건은 지난 밤 어느 늦은 시각에 일어났습니다. 경찰은 강도들이 어떻게 잡히지 않고 박물관 안으로 들어갔는지 전혀 단서를 잡지 못하고 있습니다. 그 다이아몬드는 같은 종류 중 가장 큰 것이며 매우, 매우 값비싼 것입니다. 현장에 있는 한 경찰관은 이 사건을 해결할 전문가들을 개입시킬 생각을 하고 있다고 말했습니다.

① **M** Are you planning to go to university?

W Yes. I start classes this fall.

② **W** Why are you packing your bags?

M I'm going on a trip this weekend.

③ **M** Welcome to Seasons Hostel. Can I help you?

W Yes, I'd like to book a private room.

④ **W** When would you like to leave?

M We can go after breakfast.

⑤ **M** I've always wanted to climb Mt. Everest.

W Do you want to go mountain climbing this weekend?

① **남** 너 대학에 진학할 계획이니?

여 응. 이번 가을에 수업을 시작해.

② **여** 왜 가방을 싸고 있니?

남 이번 주말에 여행 가거든.

③ **남** Seasons Hostel입니다. 도와드릴까요?

여 네. 개인 욕실이 있는 방을 예약하고 싶어요.

④ **여** 언제 떠나고 싶으세요?

남 아침을 먹고 가죠.

⑤ **남** 난 항상 Everest 산을 오르고 싶었어.

여 이번 주말에 등산 갈래?

UNIT XI ARE YOU WITH ME?

😊 Check Up

01 c **02** 1.F 2.F 3.T

03 **A** It's good to spend your money wisely. Do you <u>know what I mean</u>?

B No, I'm afraid <u>I don't get it</u>.

A All I mean is, be careful how much you spend. <u>Are you with me</u>?

B Oh, OK. <u>I get it now</u>.

Check Up Scripts

01

W Please help me find my lost kitten! I don't understand how he escaped, but he is missing. He has mostly white fur, with some black spots on his nose and ears. If you see him, reply to this ad by calling me, Lisa, at 555-9010.

여 잃어버린 새끼 고양이를 찾도록 도와주세요! 고양이가 어떻게 빠져나갔는지 모르겠는데 실종되었어요. 제 고양이는 털이 대부분 흰색이고 코와 귀에 약간 검은 점이 있어요. 제 고양이를 보시면 이 광고에 답해 주세요. Lisa에게 555-9010으로 전화 주세요.

Vocabulary	kitten 새끼 고양이 escape 탈출하다 missing 실종된 fur 털 spot 점. 얼룩 reply 응답하다 ad 광고(= advertisement)

02

M To fix your computer, you have to use anti-virus software.

W But I don't know how to do that.

M OK. First, find the software online and get it. Are you following?

W Yes, now I got it. Then what?

M Just use the software. It will tell you the problem.

W Thanks, I understand now.

남 네 컴퓨터를 고치려면 바이러스 치료 소프트웨어를 사용해야 해.

여 하지만 그걸 어떻게 하는지 몰라.

남 좋아. 우선 온라인으로 그 소프트웨어를 찾아서 받아. 내 말 이해하겠어?

여 응. 이제 알겠어. 그 다음엔 어떻게 해?

남 그냥 그 소프트웨어를 사용해. 그게 문제가 뭔지 알려줄 거야.

여 고마워. 이제 이해하겠다.

Vocabulary	fix 고치다 anti-virus 바이러스를 치료하는 software 소프트웨어

03

A It's good to spend your money wisely. Do you know what I mean?

B No, I'm afraid I don't get it.

A All I mean is, be careful how much you spend. Are you with me?

B Oh, OK. I get it now.

A 돈을 현명하게 사용하는 것이 좋아. 내 말 뜻 알겠니?

B 아니. 미안하지만 잘 모르겠어.

A 내 말은. 얼마나 많은 돈을 쓰는지 유의하라는 거야. 무슨 말인지 알겠니?

B 오, 그래. 이제 알겠다.

Vocabulary	spend (돈을) 쓰다 wisely 현명하게 get 이해하다(= understand) careful 신중한

Actual Test

1 ②　2 ③　3 ④　4 ①　5 ③　6 ②　7 ⑤　8 ④ | p.68

1

M I'm really sorry for breaking your computer.

W Don't worry; it's no big deal.

M Are you sure? I don't quite get that.

W Well, I have a warranty. That means I can replace it for free. Do you follow?

M Oh, I get it. Well, even so, I apologize for being careless.

남 네 컴퓨터를 고장 내서 정말 미안해.

여 걱정 마. 별일 아니야.

남 정말이야? 그 말 이해 못하겠는데.

여 음. 품질 보증이 있어. 그 말은 내가 무상으로 제품을 교체할 수 있다는 뜻이야. 무슨 말인지 알겠어?

남 오. 알겠다. 음. 그렇더라도 부주의했던 것 사과할게.

| Vocabulary | break 망가뜨리다　big deal 큰일　warranty 품질 보증　replace 교체하다　for free 무료로　apologize 사과하다
careless 부주의한 |

2

W Sign language gives deaf people the power to speak their minds. And when you learn, you'll be able to speak back. Today in class we are going to learn the sign for book. It's quite simple, really. Put your hands together, with your elbows down. Then open your hands as you would a real book. Are you following me? Great!

여 수화 언어는 청각 장애인들에게 마음을 표현할 수 있는 힘을 줍니다. 그리고 당신이 (그것을) 배우면 대꾸를 할 수도 있을 것입니다. 오늘 수업에서는 책을 나타내는 수화를 배워보겠습니다. 그건 사실 아주 간단합니다. 손을 모으시고 팔꿈치를 아래로 향하게 하세요. 그리고 나서 진짜 책을 펼치는 것처럼 손을 펼치세요. 이해하시겠어요? 좋습니다!

| Vocabulary | sign language 수화 언어　deaf 귀가 들리지 않는　speak back 대꾸하다　elbow 팔꿈치 |

3

W Hi, Mr. Wilkes. If you have time, I need to speak with you.

M Sure. What would you like to talk about?

W Some of the girls at the school have been bullying me.

M I'm sorry to hear that. Don't let it bother you, and they will stop. You understand?

W I don't quite get it.

M If you don't react, they'll probably get bored and quit.

W I get it. Thanks, I'll try that. See you next class.

여 안녕하세요. Wilkes 선생님. 시간 있으시면 말씀 좀 나누고 싶은데요.

남 그럼. 무슨 일로 이야기하고 싶니?

여 학교에서 몇몇 여자애들이 저를 괴롭히고 있어요.

남 그 말을 들으니 안됐구나. 그것이 널 괴롭게 하지 않도록 해. 그러면 그 애들이 그만할 거야. 무슨 말인지 알겠니?

여 잘 모르겠어요.

남 네가 반응하지 않으면 그 애들은 지루해져서 그만둘 거야.

여 알겠어요. 감사합니다. 그렇게 한번 해볼게요. 다음 수업에서 봐요.

| Vocabulary | bully 따돌리고 괴롭히다　advice 조언, 충고　bother 괴롭게 하다　react 반응하다　quit 그만두다　try 한번 해보다 |

46

M Lisa, I hate to say this, but I suspect that you cheated on your test.

W I don't get it! What makes you say so?

M You marked the same answers as the student beside you.

W Don't blame me. It's probably just an accident.

M I also know that student is your best friend, Monica.

W Sure, but we would never cheat on a test.

M I'll let this go for now. But if I catch you, you will fail the class. Is that clear?

W Yes, sir. I understand.

남 Lisa. 이 말을 하기는 싫지만 네가 시험에서 부정행위를 한 것으로 의심이 된다.

여 무슨 말씀인지 모르겠네요! 왜 그렇게 말씀하시는거죠?

남 넌 네 옆에 앉은 학생과 똑같은 답안을 작성했어.

여 저를 비난하지 마세요. 그냥 우연일 수도 있잖아요.

남 나는 또한 그 학생이 너와 가장 친한 친구인 Monica 라는 것도 알고 있지.

여 그래요. 하지만 저희는 시험에서 절대 부정행위를 하지 않아요.

남 이번은 그냥 넘어가마. 하지만 내가 널 적발하게 되면 넌 수업에서 낙제할 거야. 분명히 알아들었니?

여 네. 선생님. 알겠어요.

Vocabulary	suspect 의심하다 cheat 부정행위를 하다 accuse 비난하다, 혐의를 제기하다 mark 표시하다 beside ~ 옆에 blame 비난하다, 탓하다 accident 우연

M What a crazy morning it was for Helen! She was supposed to catch an early flight at 8:00, but her car got a flat tire on the way. After that was fixed, she arrived two hours late to the airport. She found a flight that was leaving in an hour, so she approached the ticket counter to speak with an attendant. In this situation, what will Helen likely say to the attendant?

남 Helen은 얼마나 정신 없는 아침을 보냈던가! 그녀는 8시에 출발하는 이른 비행기를 타기로 되어 있었다. 그런데 가는 길에 자동차 바퀴에 펑크가 났다. 그것을 수습하고 나서 그녀는 두 시간 늦게 공항에 도착했다. 그녀는 한 시간 후에 떠나는 항공편을 찾았다. 그래서 발권대로 다가가 직원에게 말을 건넸다. 이런 상황에서 Helen은 그 직원에게 뭐라고 말할까?

Vocabulary	be supposed to ~하기로 되어 있다 flight 비행기, 항공편 get a flat tire 바퀴에 펑크가 나다 approach 다가가다 attendant 직원, 승무원 confirm 확인하다 reservation 예약

M Mom, I'm going out to see my friends.

W Did you clean your room like I asked?

M No, I'll do it later.

W You'll do it now, young man. I asked you hours ago.

M I just don't want to. Why should I?

W It's your job to take good care of your things.

M But why now? I don't get it.

남 엄마. 저 친구들 만나러 나가요.

여 내가 부탁한 대로 방 청소는 했니?

남 아니오. 나중에 할게요.

여 지금 해야 할 거다. 얘야. 내가 몇 시간 전에 부탁했잖니.

남 그냥 하기 싫어요. 왜 해야 해요?

여 네 물건을 잘 관리하는 게 네 일이니까.

남 하지만 왜 지금요? 이해 못하겠어요.

W Because if you don't, I'll <u>ground</u> you for a week. <u>Is that clear?</u>

M Yes, Mom.

W And don't <u>argue</u> <u>with</u> me again, or it'll be two weeks.

Vocabulary	take care of ~을 돌보다, 관리하다 ground 외출을 금지시키다 argue 따지다, 말다툼하다

[The answering machine beeps.]

W Hello, this is Mrs. White. I teach <u>your</u> <u>son</u> <u>Harry</u> at the middle school. He hasn't <u>turned</u> <u>in</u> <u>his</u> <u>homework</u> for over a week. If this keeps happening, he might <u>fail</u> <u>my</u> <u>class</u>. And he may also be <u>turned</u> <u>down</u> for going to the next grade level. <u>Is that all clear?</u> Um, the time now is 9:15. I guess I'll <u>call</u> <u>back</u> in an hour to try and speak with you then. Thank you.

[자동응답기 소리]

여 안녕하세요. 저는 White 선생님입니다. 저는 중학교에서 댁의 아들 Harry를 가르칩니다. 그는 일주일이 넘도록 숙제를 제출하지 않고 있습니다. 이 일이 계속된다면 그는 제 수업을 낙제할 수 있습니다. 그리고 다음 학년으로 진급하는 것을 거절당할 수도 있습니다. 분명히 이해하셨나요? 음. 지금 시각은 9시 15분입니다. 제가 한 시간 후에 다시 전화해서 그때 통화하도록 해보겠습니다. 감사합니다.

Vocabulary	turn in 제출하다 fail 낙제하다 turn down 거절하다 grade level 학년 call back 다시 전화를 걸다

M Donna, I want to <u>apologize</u> <u>for</u> what happened.

W It was very rude of you to <u>make</u> <u>jokes</u> about me.

M I know, and I am very, very sorry.

W You <u>embarrassed</u> <u>me</u> in front of the whole class. Why would you do that?

M I just wasn't thinking. You know <u>what</u> <u>I</u> <u>mean</u>?

W Well, I still don't get it. But I think I <u>can</u> <u>forgive</u> <u>you</u>.

M Can we agree to be friends again?

W I <u>suppose</u> <u>so</u>. Promise never to do that to me again, OK?

M You <u>have</u> <u>my</u> <u>word</u>.

여 왜냐하면 지금 하지 않으면 내가 일주일 동안 외출 금지령을 내릴 테니까. 내 말 분명히 이해했니?

남 네, 엄마.

여 그리고 엄마한테 또 말대꾸하지 마. 안 그러면 2주가 될 거다.

남 Donna. 지난 일에 대해 사과하고 싶어.

여 네가 나에 대해 농담한 건 정말 무례했어.

남 알아. 그리고 정말, 정말 미안해.

여 넌 반 학생 전체 앞에서 나를 창피하게 만들었어. 왜 그런 거니?

남 그냥 아무 생각이 없었어. 내 말 무슨 뜻인지 알겠니?

여 음, 아직도 이해 못하겠어. 하지만 용서해 줄 수는 있을 것 같아.

남 그럼 우리 다시 친구가 되기로 하는 거야?

여 그러지 뭐. 다시는 나한테 그러지 않겠다고 약속해. 알겠어?

남 약속할게.

Vocabulary	apologize for ~에 대해 사과하다 happen 일어나다 rude 무례한 make jokes 농담을 하다 embarrass 창피[당황]하게 하다 forgive 용서하다 suppose 추측하다 promise 약속하다 You have my word. 약속해. make fun of ~을 놀리다

UNIT XII WHAT DO YOU MEAN?

Check Up

01 b **02** b

03 **A** Wasn't he on the baseball team last year?

B You mean the guy over there wearing a sports jersey?

A Yes, I think that's the pitcher. He really brought the heat, didn't he?

B What do you mean by that?

A Oh, it means he was a very good pitcher.

Check Up Scripts

01

a. **M** Let's go to the museum.
   W OK. I like to look at paintings.

b. **M** That's a mummy, isn't it?
   W Yes, and it is very ancient.

c. **M** Would you like to see a mummy?
   W No, thank you. They're scary.

a. **남** 박물관에 가자.
   여 그래. 나는 그림 보는 걸 좋아해.

b. **남** 저건 미라 아니야?
   여 맞아. 그리고 아주 오래된 거야.

c. **남** 미라 보고 싶어?
   여 아니, 됐어. 미라는 무서워.

> Vocabulary museum 박물관 painting 그림 mummy 미라 ancient 오래된, 고대의 scary 무서운

02

W I like your new shoes, Max.

M Thanks. They look great, but they really hurt my feet.

W As they say, "All that glitters is not gold."

M What does that mean?

W It means some things that look pretty may not be so great after all.

여 네 새 신발 맘에 든다. Max.

남 고마워. 모양이 멋지지. 그런데 발을 너무 아프게 해.

여 사람들 말처럼 "반짝이는 것이 모두 금은 아닌"거지.

남 그게 무슨 말이야?

여 예뻐 보이는 것들이 결국에는 그렇게 좋은 게 아닐 수도 있다는 뜻이야.

> Vocabulary hurt 아프게 하다 glitter 반짝이다 after all 결국

03

A Wasn't he on the baseball team last year?

B You mean the guy over there wearing a sports jersey?

A Yes, I think that's the pitcher. He really brought the heat, didn't he?

B What do you mean by that?

A Oh, it means he was a very good pitcher.

A 저 남자 작년에 야구 팀에 있지 않았어?

B 스포츠용 스웨터를 입은 저 남자 말이야?

A 응. 그 투수인 것 같아. 그는 정말 끝내줬는데, 그렇지 않았어?

B 그게 무슨 말이야?

A 아, 그가 정말 훌륭한 투수였다는 말이야.

> Vocabulary baseball 야구 sports jersey 스포츠용 스웨터 pitcher 투수

Actual Test

1 ② 2 ④ 3 ③ 4 ② 5 ③ 6 ④ 7 ⑤ 8 ④

| p.74

1

M Can you tell me the way to the grocery store?

W Of course. Go north on Lake Street. Then turn left onto Park Road.

M OK. What do I do then?

W You will pass the city park on your left. Then take the next right.

M You mean turn onto Mill Street?

W Yes, exactly. The grocery store will be on the right.

M Great. Thanks so much for the help!

남 식료품점에 가는 길 좀 가르쳐 주시겠어요?

여 그럼요. Lake Street를 따라 북쪽으로 가세요. 그러고 나서 Park Road로 좌회전하세요.

남 네. 그 다음에는 어떻게 하죠?

여 왼쪽에 시립 공원을 지나치실 거예요. 그러고 난 다음에 우회전하세요.

남 Mill Street로 돌라는 말씀이신가요?

여 네, 바로 그거예요. 식료품점은 오른쪽에 있을 거예요.

남 좋아요. 도와주셔서 정말 감사합니다!

> **Vocabulary** grocery store 식료품점 pass ~을 지나다 exactly 정확히

2

W Can I help you, sir?

M Yes, I have a package to send.

W OK. Would you like to overnight it?

M What do you mean?

W It means the package will arrive tomorrow.

M That sounds fine. Is it expensive?

W A bit. You'll need a special stamp.

M OK, I suppose it's worth it.

W We'll ship this out tonight, sir.

여 도와드릴까요, 손님?

남 네. 소포를 보내야 해서요.

여 알겠습니다. 익일 배송을 하실 건가요?

남 무슨 뜻이죠?

여 소포가 내일 도착한다는 뜻입니다.

남 그게 좋겠네요. 비싼가요?

여 조금요. 특별한 우표가 필요해요.

남 알겠습니다. 그만한 가치가 있겠죠.

여 오늘 밤에 발송하겠습니다.

> **Vocabulary** package 소포 arrive 도착하다 stamp 우표 suppose 추측하다 be worth it 그럴 가치가 있다
> ship 발송하다

3

W Have you begun your final essay, Simon?

M Yes, Maria. I started last night. It's going to be tough.

W What does that mean?

M Oh, it's a way of saying something is difficult.

W I see. Well, then my essay will be tough as well.

M I'm writing about the French Revolution.

여 기말 에세이 시작했니, Simon?

남 응, Maria. 어젯밤에 시작했어. 힘들 것 같아.

여 무슨 뜻이니?

남 아, 무언가가 어렵다고 말하는 한 방법이야.

여 알겠다. 음, 그럼 내 에세이도 힘들겠다.

남 난 프랑스 대혁명에 대해 쓰고 있어.

50

W	That's exciting. I'm writing about Spanish history.	여	흥미롭네. 나는 스페인 역사에 대해 쓰려고 해.
M	Your family comes from Spain, right?	남	너희 가족이 스페인에서 왔지?
W	Yes, I want to learn more about my heritage.	여	응. 나는 우리 전통에 대해서 더 많은 것을 배우고 싶어.

> Vocabulary tough 힘든, 어려운   as well 역시, 또한   revolution 혁명   heritage 전통, 유산

4

W	Once upon a time, there was an evil queen with magic powers. She lived in a large kingdom far, far away from here. One day, she asked her magic mirror, "Aren't I the most beautiful woman of all?" But the magic mirror told her that there was a girl much more beautiful than she. The queen became angry, and cast a spell to make the prettier girl sleep forever.	여	옛날 옛적에 마법의 힘을 가진 사악한 왕비가 살았어요. 그녀는 여기서 아주 아주 멀리 떨어진 커다란 왕국에서 살았어요. 어느 날. 그녀는 마법의 거울에게 물었어요. "내가 모든 여자들 중에서 제일 아름답지 않니?" 하지만 마법의 거울은 그녀보다 훨씬 더 아름다운 소녀가 있다고 말했어요. 왕비는 분노해서 그 더 예쁜 소녀를 영원히 잠들게 하는 마법을 걸었어요.

> Vocabulary evil 사악한   magic 마법의   kingdom 왕국   mirror 거울   cast a spell 마법을 걸다

5

W	Do you know the story of Amelia Earhart?	여	너 Amelia Earhart 이야기 아니?
M	Yes. She was a pilot, wasn't she?	남	응. 비행기 조종사 아니었니?
W	She was. She disappeared over a century ago.	여	맞아. 그녀는 백 년도 더 전에 사라졌어.
M	She tried to fly around the world, but never made it across the Pacific Ocean.	남	그녀는 세계 일주 비행을 하려고 했는데 태평양을 영영 건너지 못했지.
W	Yes, it's quite a mystery. No one knows what happened.	여	맞아. 그건 정말 미스터리야. 무슨 일이 일어났는지 아무도 몰라.
M	Didn't she hold a world record?	남	그녀는 세계 기록을 갖고 있지 않니?
W	In fact, she did. The first woman to fly alone across the Atlantic.	여	사실 그랬어. 혼자서 대서양을 횡단한 최초의 여성이었지.
M	Wow, you sure know a lot about the subject.	남	와, 너 그 주제에 대해서 정말 많이 아는구나.
W	I read a great book about it. I can let you borrow it if you like.	여	그것에 대한 좋은 책을 읽었거든. 원한다면 너에게 빌려줄게.

> Vocabulary pilot 비행기 조종사   disappear 사라지다   century 1세기, 백 년   make it 도착하다. 약속을 지키다
> the Pacific (Ocean) 태평양   mystery 미스터리   world record 세계 기록   the Atlantic (Ocean) 대서양
> crash (비행기가) 추락하다

6

	[The answering machine beeps.]		[자동응답기 소리]
W	This message is for Ms. Lee. I'm calling	여	이 메시지는 이 씨에게 남기는 것입니다. Dale's 세탁

from Dale's Dry Cleaning to tell you that your clothes are ready. You had one dress for $2, two sweaters for $5 each, an overcoat that cost $5, and four blouses for $12 altogether. You can pick them up anytime this afternoon. Thanks again for your business.

소인데요. 손님 옷들이 준비되었다는 걸 알려드리려고요. 손님께서는 2달러에 드레스 한 벌, 각각 5달러에 스웨터 두 벌, 5달러에 오버코트 한 벌, 그리고 합쳐서 12달러에 블라우스 네 벌을 맡기셨습니다. 오늘 오후 아무 때나 찾아가실 수 있습니다. 저희 세탁소를 이용해 주셔서 다시 한 번 감사드립니다.

Vocabulary	overcoat 오버코트 pick up 찾아가다

① M This is a new car you're driving, isn't it?

W Yes, I just bought it on Saturday.

② M Jina and I met back in elementary school.

W That was more than a decade ago.

③ M What does that new painting at the museum mean?

W I don't know. It's so hard to tell with modern art.

④ M Is this the correct spelling of "acheive"?

W Um, no. The *i* comes before the *e*, I think.

⑤ M That's amazing! The robot looks almost like a human.

W No, I don't think most robots are very advanced.

① 남 이건 네가 운전하는 새 차 아니니?

여 맞아. 토요일에 막 구입했어.

② 남 지나와 나는 초등학교 때 만났어.

여 그럼 10년도 더 전이었군요.

③ 남 박물관에 새로 걸린 그림은 어떤 의미일까?

여 모르겠어. 현대 미술은 이해하기가 너무 어려워.

④ 여 이게 "acheive"의 올바른 철자 맞니?

남 음. 아니야. i가 e보다 먼저 와야 하는 것 같아.

⑤ 남 굉장하다! 저 로봇은 거의 사람처럼 보여.

여 아니야. 나는 대부분의 로봇들이 별로 발전되지 않았다고 생각해.

Vocabulary	college 대학 decade 10년 modern 현대의 correct 올바른, 정확한 spelling 철자 achieve 성취하다
	amazing 굉장한 advanced 발전한

M The Mongol Empire, um, led by Genghis Khan, covered most of Asia and parts of Europe, too. That makes it the largest in history, doesn't it? It lasted for a few hundred years. Many battles were fought to get new lands and keep old ones. But after the death of Genghis Khan, the empire began to break up. His sons could not rule them successfully. Within a century, the great empire crumbled.

남 몽골 제국은, 음. Genghis Khan에 의해 이끌어졌는데 아시아의 대부분과 유럽의 일부분을 포함했습니다. 그러니까 역사상 가장 큰 제국이었던 거죠, 그렇지 않나요? 그것은 수백 년 동안 지속되었습니다. 새로운 영토를 획득하고 예전 영토를 지키기 위해 많은 전투가 치뤄졌습니다. 하지만 Genghis Khan의 사후에 제국은 분열되기 시작합니다. 그의 아들들은 성공적으로 제국들을 통치하지 못했습니다. 한 세기가 지나기 전에 그 위대한 제국은 무너지고 말았습니다.

Vocabulary	empire 제국 cover 포함하다 battle 전투 break up 분열되다 rule 통치하다 successfully 성공적으로
	crumble 무너지다

모의고사 1회

01 ④	02 ④	03 ②	04 ②	05 ⑤	06 ①	07 ⑤	08 ④	09 ③	10 ④
11 ③	12 ①	13 ②	14 ①	15 ④	16 ④	17 ③	18 ①	19 ⑤	20 ④

01

M The heat this summer is just awful!

W I know. I don't think it's ever been this hot. It makes me sweat like crazy!

M It was a great idea to come to the pool.

W I agree with you. There's no better way to cool off on a hot summer day.

M And it's great exercise! I'm going to the diving board.

남 이번 여름의 열기는 정말 끔찍하네!

여 알아. 이렇게 더웠던 적이 없었던 것 같아. 미친 듯이 땀을 흘리게 돼!

남 수영장에 오기로 한 건 정말 좋은 생각이었어.

여 나도 그렇게 생각해. 더운 여름날 열기를 식히기에 이보다 좋은 방법이 없지.

남 그리고 좋은 운동이기도 하고! 난 다이빙 보드에 가야겠어.

02

W Hi, Paul. Can you do me a favor?

M Sure, what is it?

W Well, I have a big report due tomorrow.

M For social studies class, right?

W That's the one. But I can't locate my textbook.

M Would you like me to help you find it?

W Actually, I was hoping I could borrow yours.

M Of course. But I need it back in the morning.

W Thanks so much, Paul.

여 안녕, Paul. 부탁 하나 들어줄 수 있어?

남 그럼, 뭔데 그래?

여 음, 내가 내일까지 써야 하는 중요한 보고서가 있거든.

남 사회 수업에 낼 거 맞지?

여 바로 그거야. 그런데 내 교과서가 어디 있는지 모르겠어.

남 찾는 걸 도와줄까?

여 사실은 네 걸 빌릴 수 있을까 하고 있었어.

남 물론이지. 하지만 내일 아침에 돌려받아야 해.

여 정말 고마워, Paul.

03

M Today, my mother and I visited a Buddhist temple. It was really nice of her to take me out for the day. The temple was really beautiful, and very old too. The big statue of the Buddha was the coolest thing we saw. It was fat and golden. People left gifts there. We also watched the monks perform a special ceremony. It was a great day.

남 오늘, 엄마와 나는 절에 갔었다. 엄마가 오늘 나를 데려가신 것은 정말 고마운 일이었다. 절은 매우 아름다웠고 매우 오래되기도 했다. 커다란 불상은 우리가 본 가장 멋진 것이었다. 그것은 풍채가 좋고 금빛이었다. 사람들은 그곳에 선물을 남겨두었다. 우리는 또 스님들이 특별한 의식을 행하는 것을 지켜보았다. 굉장한 날이었다.

04

W ① The nurse is talking with a sick patient.

② The doctor is examining a young patient.

③ The surgeon is operating on a young girl.

④ The patient is having an argument with the doctor.

⑤ The patient is taking medicine from the doctor.

여 ① 간호사가 아픈 환자와 이야기를 하고 있다.

② 의사가 어린 환자를 진찰하고 있다.

③ 외과 의사가 어린 여자아이에게 수술을 하고 있다.

④ 환자가 의사와 말다툼을 하고 있다.

⑤ 환자가 의사로부터 약을 받고 있다.

05

M In today's news, fewer people will be traveling for vacation this year. With so many people having money problems, this comes as no surprise. Most people report that their budget simply does not allow it. Instead of travel, many families are visiting local attractions near their own hometowns. They call it a "staycation." It saves money, and still allows families to have fun together.

남 오늘의 소식입니다. 올해에는 더 적은 수의 사람들이 휴가 때 여행을 떠나겠습니다. 많은 사람들이 금전적인 문제를 겪고 있기에 놀라운 소식은 아닙니다. 대부분의 사람들은 그들의 예산이 그것[여행]을 허락하지 않는다고 말했습니다. 여행을 떠나는 대신 많은 가족들은 그들이 사는 곳에서 가까운 지역 명소를 방문하고 있습니다. 그것을 "staycation"이라고 부릅니다. 그것은 돈을 절약하게 해주면서도 가족들이 함께 즐거운 시간을 보내도록 해줍니다.

06

W Would you like to go see a movie on Saturday?

M No, I'm afraid I can't. I'm going to visit my grandfather this weekend.

W Really? Where does he live?

M He lives on the coast. We have to take the train there.

W That's a long way, isn't it?

M It is quite a long journey, yes. But I love spending time with him.

W How long will you stay?

M Only a few days. I'll be back for school on Monday.

여 토요일에 영화 보러 갈래?

남 아니, 안 되겠어. 이번 주말에 할아버지 댁에 가려고 하거든.

여 정말? 어디 사시는데?

남 해안 지방에 사셔. 우린 기차를 타고 거기로 가야 해.

여 먼 길이지, 그렇지 않니?

남 상당히 먼 여행이야, 맞아. 하지만 나는 할아버지와 함께 시간을 보내는 게 정말 좋아.

여 얼마나 오래 머물 거니?

남 며칠만. 난 월요일에 다시 학교에 갈 거야.

07

M I can't wait until I graduate from high school. I'm going straight to university to study biology. I love to study how plants and animals live and breathe. It's fascinating. Of course, what I really want to be is a doctor.

남 나는 고등학교를 졸업할 때가 너무 기다려진다. 나는 곧장 대학에 가서 생물학을 공부할 것이다. 나는 식물과 동물이 어떻게 살아가고 호흡하는지 공부하는 것이 정말 좋다. 그건 정말 흥미롭다. 물론 내가 정말 되고 싶은 것은 의사이다. 그래서 나는 그 후에 대학 공부를 몇 년 더 할 것이다. 내

So I'll have a few more years of university after that. My biggest dream is that one day I can cure a disease. I want my name in the history books.

가장 큰 꿈은 언젠가 질병을 치료하는 것이다. 나는 역사책에 내 이름이 실리기를 바란다.

08

[The telephone rings.]

M This is Mr. Meyer's office. How can I help you?

W Is Mr. Meyer in, please?

M No, I'm sorry. I can take a message though.

W Just tell him that Susan Green called.

M And what is it about?

W We have a business meeting today.

M OK. What time would that be?

W He should arrive at 4:00, in conference room A.

M And what's your call back number?

W It's 555-7634.

M Thank you, ma'am. I'll pass this along.

[전화벨 소리]

남 Meyer 씨의 사무실입니다. 무엇을 도와드릴까요?

여 Meyer 씨 계신가요?

남 아니오. 죄송합니다. 하지만 메시지를 남기실 수 있습니다.

여 그냥 Susan Green이 전화했다고만 전해주세요.

남 용건은 무엇인가요?

여 오늘 사업상 미팅이 있습니다.

남 알겠습니다. 시간이 언제인가요?

여 그는 4시 정각까지 회의실 A에 도착해야 합니다.

남 다시 전화드릴 번호는 어떻게 되나요?

여 555-7634입니다.

남 감사합니다. 메시지를 전달하겠습니다.

09

W Hi, Charlie. You look down. What's the problem?

M I'm really getting fed up with my classes this year.

W I know how you feel. Mine are hard too.

M There is so much homework, and so little time to do it.

W Besides that, we have all those presentations to give.

M And all the essays! I've written 10 already.

W I can't wait for it to be over. Just a few more weeks until summer.

M Yeah. I could really use some time off.

여 안녕. Charlie. 너 기분이 좀 안 좋아 보인다. 무슨 일 있어?

남 난 올해 수업들에 정말 질리고 있어.

여 네 기분이 어떤지 알아. 내 수업들도 어려워.

남 숙제가 너무 많은데 그걸 할 시간은 너무 적어.

여 게다가. 우린 그 모든 발표도 해야 하잖아.

남 그리고 그 모든 에세이들! 난 벌 써 10편을 썼어.

여 빨리 끝났으면 좋겠어. 몇 주만 더 있으면 여름이야.

남 그래. 정말 쉴 시간을 좀 갖고 싶어.

10

W Welcome to Ocean Airlines. How can I help you?

M I'd like to buy a ticket to Boston, please.

W OK. The ticket will cost $400.

여 Ocean Airlines에 오신 것을 환영합니다. 무엇을 도와드릴까요?

남 Boston 행 표를 사고 싶습니다.

여 알겠습니다. 표 값은 400달러입니다.

M That is roundtrip, isn't it?

W Yes, sir. But it doesn't include taxes and fees.

M What do you mean?

W Taxes will add an additional $50. How many bags do you have?

M I have two bags.

W OK. We also charge $20 per bag.

M I guess that's fine. Can you confirm the price?

남 왕복이죠, 그렇죠?

여 네, 그렇습니다. 하지만 세금과 수수료는 포함되지 않은 가격입니다.

남 무슨 뜻인가요?

여 세금으로 50달러가 추가로 붙을 것입니다. 가방이 몇 개인가요?

남 두 개입니다.

여 알겠습니다. 저희는 가방당 20달러를 부과합니다.

남 괜찮은 것 같네요. 가격을 확인해 주시겠어요?

11

W Marla has always been a great artist. She loves to draw, paint, and sculpt. So when she graduated high school, naturally she wanted to go to art school. But the price was so expensive! She knew she couldn't afford it, but she applied to art schools anyway. She almost gave up, but one day she got a phone call from a school. They said they would love to have her study there. She mentioned that she couldn't afford it. To her surprise, the man said they could give her a full scholarship! She couldn't pass up such a great opportunity. In this situation, what is Marla likely to say to the man?

여 Marla는 언제나 훌륭한 예술가였다. 그녀는 그림을 그리고, 색을 칠하고, 조각하는 것을 정말 좋아한다. 그래서 고등학교를 졸업했을 때 그녀는 자연스럽게 예술 학교에 가고 싶었다. 하지만 학비가 너무 비쌌다! 그녀는 그 돈을 낼 수 없다는 걸 알았지만 어쨌든 예술 학교들에 지원했다. 그녀는 거의 포기했는데 어느 날 한 학교에서 전화를 받았다. 그들은 그녀가 그곳에서 공부하기를 원한다고 했다. 그녀는 돈을 낼 수 없다고 말했다. 놀랍게도, 그 남자는 학교 측에서 그녀에게 전액 장학금을 줄 수 있다고 했다! 그녀는 그런 좋은 기회를 보낼 수 없었다. 이런 상황에서 Marla는 그 남자에게 뭐라고 말하겠는가?

12

M Hey, Jan. Would you like to go to the mall with me this weekend?

W I don't think so. I really don't like the mall.

M Why? What's the problem?

W It's just so crowded and loud all the time.

M Would you prefer a quieter place instead?

W Yeah. How about the park?

M Sure, we can hang out at the park.

W Great, I'll see you there.

남 안녕, Jan. 이번 주말에 나랑 같이 쇼핑몰에 갈래?

여 안 될 것 같아. 난 쇼핑몰을 별로 좋아하지 않거든.

남 왜? 뭐가 문제인데?

여 그냥 거기는 항상 너무 붐비고 시끄러워서.

남 그럼 대신 더 조용한 곳이 좋을까?

여 그래. 공원은 어때?

남 좋지. 공원에서 놀 수 있겠다.

여 좋았어. 거기서 보자.

13

M This morning, I got some awful news. The city is planning to build a parking lot over a local nature preserve. When I read it in the

남 오늘 아침, 저는 끔찍한 소식을 들었습니다. 시에서 지역의 자연보호 구역에 주차장을 건설할 계획이라는 것입니다. 그것을 신문에서 읽었을 때 저는 소리지르지 않을 수 없

paper, I couldn't help but shout. I couldn't believe it! How could they do such a thing? I just kept thinking of all the plants and wildlife that will be destroyed. There are too few natural areas in the city as it is. Why destroy another? So I am planning to write a letter to the mayor.

었습니다. 믿을 수가 없었습니다! 어떻게 그런 짓을 할 수가 있죠? 전 그저 파괴될 모든 식물들과 야생 생물들에 대해 계속 생각할 뿐이었습니다. 지금 시에는 자연이 있는 지역이 너무 적습니다. 왜 또 하나를 파괴하는 것입니까? 그래서 저는 시장에게 편지를 쓰려고 합니다.

14

W Hi, Mark. What's the matter?

M I think I might need a part-time job.

W Why do you say that?

M Now that I can drive, my father wants me to pay for gas.

W At least you have your own transportation.

M But a job might lower my grades in school.

W I don't think so. I know plenty of people who work a few hours on the weekends.

M And they still have good grades?

W Of course! It's really not that hard.

여 안녕. Mark. 무슨 일 있니?

남 아르바이트 자리가 필요할 것 같아서.

여 왜 그런 말을 하니?

남 이제 내가 운전을 하니까 아빠가 나보고 기름값을 내라고 하셔.

여 적어도 넌 너만의 교통수단이 있긴 하네.

남 하지만 일을 하면 성적이 낮아질지도 몰라.

여 난 그렇게 생각하지 않아. 주말에 몇 시간 동안 일을 하는 사람들을 많이 알고 있어.

남 그리고 그들은 여전히 좋은 성적을 받고?

여 물론이지! 그건 그렇게 어려운 일이 아니야.

15

M Look around you. Kids today face different challenges than their parents and grandparents. You live in a quickly changing world, and it can be difficult to keep up. Not to mention, it might be harder to get a job when you graduate. You have a lot of important things to think about while in school. But don't worry about it too much. Stay positive, and find your own happiness. That's really all that matters.

남 주위를 둘러보세요. 오늘날 어린이들은 그들의 부모나 조부모와는 다른 도전에 직면하고 있습니다. 여러분은 빠르게 변화하는 세상에 살고 있고 속도를 맞추기가 어려울 수 있습니다. 말할 것도 없이. 여러분이 졸업할 때에는 일자리를 얻기가 더 힘들 것입니다. 여러분은 학교를 다니는 동안 생각해야 할 중요한 것들이 많습니다. 하지만 너무 걱정하지는 마세요. 긍정적으로 생각하고 자신만의 행복을 찾으세요. 그것이 정말 중요한 것입니다.

16

W Excuse me, do you have a moment to chat?

M Of course, ma'am. What's the trouble?

W My car was broken into tonight.

M OK. I can help you file a report.

W That would be great. My name is Karen Wright.

여 실례합니다. 잠깐 이야기 좀 할 수 있을까요?

남 그럼요, 부인. 무슨 문제가 있으십니까?

여 제 차가 오늘 저녁에 침입을 당했어요.

남 알겠습니다. 보고서 작성을 도와드리겠습니다.

여 그러면 좋겠습니다. 제 이름은 Karen Wright입니다.

M How do you spell that?	**남** 철자를 어떻게 쓰시죠?
W W-R-I-G-H-T.	**여** W-R-I-G-H-T입니다.
M Where did the theft occur?	**남** 절도가 어디에서 일어났나요?
W In the mall parking lot.	**여** 쇼핑몰 주차장에서요.
M OK. We'll look into it for you. If we find the criminal, we'll call you.	**남** 알겠습니다. 저희가 조사하겠습니다. 범인을 찾으면 전화 드리겠습니다.
W I really appreciate it.	**여** 정말 감사합니다.

17

① **M** Are you going to the lecture tonight?	① **남** 오늘 저녁 강의에 갈 거니?
W I'd love to, but I have lots of homework.	**여** 가고 싶은데 숙제가 많아.
② **M** I shouldn't have eaten so much pizza.	② **남** 피자를 그렇게 많이 먹지 말았어야 하는데.
W Why do you say so? Do you feel sick?	**여** 왜 그렇게 말하니? 속이 안 좋아?
③ **M** It's difficult to breathe with all the pollution.	③ **남** 공해가 너무 심해서 숨쉬기가 힘들어.
W Yes, my car makes less pollution than most.	**여** 맞아. 내 차는 대부분의 차보다 공해를 적게 유발해.
④ **M** Would you like to get some sushi for dinner?	④ **남** 저녁으로 초밥 먹을래?
W Oh yes! Seafood is my favorite.	**여** 오 좋아! 해물은 내가 제일 좋아하는 거야.
⑤ **M** I'm very sorry that I caused damage to your car.	⑤ **남** 당신 차에 손상을 입혀서 정말 죄송합니다.
W It's OK. I don't think it's very serious anyway.	**여** 괜찮아요. 어쨌거나 별로 심하지도 않은 것 같은데요.

18

W Have you decided what you want yet?	**여** 뭘 드실 건지 결정하셨나요?
M I just have a few questions.	**남** 질문이 몇 개 있어요.
W Of course. Go right ahead.	**여** 그럼요. 말씀하세요.
M Is the salmon fresh? I don't like frozen seafood.	**남** 연어가 신선한가요? 전 냉동 해산물을 좋아하지 않아서요.
W Yes, the fish comes in daily.	**여** 네. 생선은 매일 들어옵니다.
M That sounds delicious. I'll take it.	**남** 맛있겠네요. 그걸 먹을게요.
W Would you like anything else, sir?	**여** 다른 것은 필요 없으신가요, 손님?
M Let me have a chef's salad on the side.	**남** 주방장 추천 샐러드를 곁들여 먹을게요.
W Sure. I'll have your order out shortly.	**여** 알겠습니다. 주문하신 요리를 곧 내오겠습니다.
M Great. Please make sure not to overcook the fish.	**남** 좋아요. 생선을 너무 익히지 않게 주의하세요.
W Of course.	**여** 물론이죠.

19

M I wish I hadn't taken the bus today.	**남** 오늘 버스를 타지 말 걸 그랬어.
W Really? Why is that?	**여** 정말? 왜?
M It's usually right on time, but today it was 10 minutes late.	**남** 보통은 제시간에 오는데 오늘은 10분 늦었지 뭐야.
W Maybe you should take a different mode of transportation. The subway is probably quicker and more reliable. I take it every day, and I'm always on time.	**여** 어쩌면 넌 다른 교통수단을 이용해야 할지도 몰라. 지하철이 아마 더 빠르고 믿을 만할 거야. 나는 매일 지하철을 타는데 항상 제시간에 오잖아.
M Well, maybe I'll try that tomorrow morning.	**남** 음. 내일 아침에 그걸 시도해 봐야겠다.
W I'd be happy to meet and ride with you if you like.	**여** 네가 원한다면 만나서 너랑 같이 타고 가도 좋겠다.

20

M Will you do me a favor, Pam?	**남** 부탁 좀 들어줄래. Pam?
W Sure. What is it?	**여** 그럼. 무슨 부탁인데?
M I have a library book that I need to return, but I'm so busy this afternoon.	**남** 반납해야 할 도서관 책이 한 권 있는데 오늘 오후에 너무 바빠.
W Would you like me to drop it off for you?	**여** 너 대신 그걸 반납해줄까?
M If you can, that would be great.	**남** 그럴 수 있다면 정말 좋겠어.
W Sure. I'm meeting with my professor at 1:00, and I'll be right next to the library.	**여** 좋아. 1시에 교수님과 만나는데 도서관 바로 옆에 있을 거야.

모의고사 2회

01 ③	**02** ④	**03** ②	**04** ③	**05** ④	**06** ②	**07** ④	**08** ⑤	**09** ②	**10** ⑤
11 ②	**12** ④	**13** ①	**14** ③	**15** ④	**16** ④	**17** ④	**18** ④	**19** ④	**20** ①

01

M How would you like to celebrate our wedding anniversary this year?	**남** 올해 우리 결혼 기념일을 어떻게 기념하고 싶어?
W We could take a weekend trip to the mountains.	**여** 산으로 주말 여행을 갈 수도 있겠다.
M We did that last year. What if we went camping?	**남** 그건 작년에 했잖아. 캠핑을 가면 어떨까?
W There's nothing romantic about camping. How about the city?	**여** 캠핑에는 낭만이 없어. 도시는 어때?

M	Too loud. Want to go out for a fancy dinner?	남	너무 시끄러워. 멋진 저녁식사 하러 외출할까?
W	Not really. But a couple of days at the beach might be relaxing.	여	별로. 하지만 해변에서 이틀 정도 보내는 건 마음을 편안하게 해줄 것 같아.
M	Yeah, I think you're right.	남	그래. 당신 말이 맞는 것 같아.

02

W	Welcome, everyone, for the grand opening of the Biggs Gallery. It's so great to see so many people here today. This is an exciting day for our community. Today we show our appreciation for the arts by opening the town's first ever public art gallery. We thank you for all your support in making this possible. Now please, have some refreshments at the door and enjoy the wonderful exhibitions inside.	여	Biggs 미술관의 개관 행사에 오신 것을 환영합니다. 여러분. 오늘 여기 이렇게 많은 분들이 오신 것을 보니 참 좋습니다. 오늘은 우리 지역사회에 있어서 설레는 날입니다. 오늘 우리는 이 도시 최초의 공립 미술관을 개관함으로써 예술에 대한 우리의 관심을 나타내게 되었습니다. 이것을 가능할 수 있도록 여러분께서 주신 모든 도움에 감사드립니다. 자. 이제 출입구 쪽에 있는 다과를 드시고 안쪽에 있는 훌륭한 전시를 즐기십시오.

03

M	Excuse me, ma'am? I think we are ready to order.	남	실례합니다? 저희 주문 좀 할게요.
W	Of course. Can I suggest the tuna? It's a popular dish.	여	물론이죠. 참치를 권해드려도 될까요? 인기가 많은 요리예요.
M	I don't think I'm in the mood for fish.	남	별로 생선을 먹을 기분이 아니라서요.
W	OK. How about one of our famous cheeseburgers?	여	알겠습니다. 저희의 유명한 치즈 버거 중 하나는 어떠세요?
M	Hmm, I don't think so. I don't eat red meat.	남	흠. 안 되겠어요. 제가 붉은 고기는 안 먹어서요.
W	OK. We have a great selection of salads, if you'd like.	여	알겠습니다. 샐러드 종류도 많이 있습니다. 원하신다면요.
M	That sounds OK. But first, how is the chicken cooked?	남	그거 괜찮네요. 하지만 먼저, 닭고기가 어떻게 요리되나요?
W	It is breaded and fried, and served with French fries.	여	빵과 함께 튀겨서 감자 튀김과 함께 나옵니다.
M	Oh, I don't eat fried foods. OK, I think the grilled chicken would be best.	남	오. 전 튀긴 음식은 먹지 않아요. 좋아요. 석쇠에 구운 닭고기가 가장 좋겠네요.

04

M	Marta, it appears that my watch is missing.	남	Marta. 내 시계가 없어진 것 같아.
W	Where did you leave it last?	여	마지막에 어디에 뒀는데?
M	I left it right here on the table just 10 minutes ago.	남	10분 전에 바로 여기 탁자 위에 놔뒀어.
W	What do you think happened to it?	여	어떻게 된 거라고 생각해?

M I don't know. What do you think?	남 모르겠어. 네 생각은 어떤데?
W You're accusing me of stealing it, aren't you?	여 너 설마 내가 훔쳤다고 생각하는 거야?
M Well, it seems like the only explanation.	남 음, 그게 유일한 설명인 것 같은데.
W I can't believe you would blame me for something like that. I would never!	여 네가 그런 걸로 날 비난하다니 믿어지지 않는다. 난 절대 그런 짓 안 해!
M It's OK, it was just an idea. Don't worry.	남 됐어. 그냥 떠오른 생각이야. 신경 쓰지 마.
W Well, it's a terrible thing to say. I don't think we should be friends.	여 음, 그건 정말 안 좋은 말이야. 우린 친구가 될 수 없을 것 같다.
M Come on, I apologized.	남 야, 내가 사과했잖아.
W It doesn't matter. You went too far.	여 상관 없어. 넌 너무 심했어.

05

M ① The kids are shopping for a pet.	남 ① 아이들이 애완동물을 사고 있다.
② The children are hiking in the jungle.	② 아이들이 정글에서 하이킹을 하고 있다.
③ The kids are camping in the forest.	③ 아이들이 숲에서 캠핑을 하고 있다.
④ The children are visiting the zoo.	④ 아이들이 동물원을 방문하고 있다.
⑤ The kids are climbing a tree.	⑤ 아이들이 나무에 오르고 있다.

06

W It's that time of year again, as the baseball season begins for yet another year. The Tigers played the Bears tonight in the year's first game. The Tigers made a great effort, scoring three home runs and three more runs after that. But it was no match for the Bears' amazing offense. They scored eight runs to win the game. All in all, it was a fun game, and a great way to start the season.	여 올해에도 그 시기가 다시 찾아왔습니다. 야구 시즌이 새로운 해를 맞아 시작됩니다. 오늘 저녁 Tigers는 Bears와 올해 첫 경기를 했습니다. Tigers는 열심히 노력해서 홈런 세 개를 쳐냈고 3점을 추가로 냈습니다. 하지만 Bears의 대단한 공격력과는 상대가 되지 않았습니다. Bears는 8점을 내서 경기에서 승리했습니다. 전체적으로 재미있는 경기였고 시즌을 시작하기에 좋은 방법이었습니다.

07

W Would you like to go to the gym with me?	여 나랑 같이 헬스 클럽에 갈래?
M Absolutely. I need to work out my muscles.	남 물론이지. 근육을 좀 단련해야 해.
W OK. I'll be free at 4:00. Is that a good time?	여 좋아. 나는 4시에 시간이 돼. 그때 괜찮아?
M I have English lessons then. What about two hours after?	남 난 그때 영어 수업이 있어. 두 시간 후는 어때?
W That's when I eat dinner with my family. How about an hour before that?	여 그때는 내가 식구들이랑 저녁을 먹을 때야. 그것보다 한 시간 전은 어때?
M That sounds fine. I'll show up then.	남 괜찮은 것 같아. 그때 갈게.

08

M I can't understand why my computer isn't working.

W Why? What's the problem?

M It turns off without any warning.

W Did you try restarting it?

M Yes. It starts just like it should, but then five minutes later it just dies.

W Have you downloaded anything lately?

M Yeah, just a little software last night. Why?

W It could be a virus. Sometimes they hide in software.

M Oh no! What do I do about it?

W It should be easy to fix. You just need some anti-virus software.

남 내 컴퓨터가 왜 작동을 안 하는지 모르겠어.

여 왜? 뭐가 문젠데?

남 아무 경고도 없이 전원이 꺼져.

여 컴퓨터를 다시 켜봤어?

남 응. 시작은 제대로 되는데 5분 후에 갑자기 꺼져버려.

여 최근에 뭐 다운로드 받은 거 있어?

남 응. 어젯밤에 그냥 작은 소프트웨어를 받았는데. 왜?

여 그게 바이러스일 수 있어. 가끔 바이러스가 소프트웨어에 숨어 있거든.

남 오 이런! 어떻게 하지?

여 고치기 쉬울 거야. 그냥 바이러스 치료 소프트웨어만 있으면 돼.

09

W I have a really fun job. If you like money, then you would love my job. People come to me all day to get help with their finances. I help them put money into and take money out of their accounts. Sometimes, I give people loans to buy cars, buy houses, and even start businesses. I love my job because I feel like a really important part of the community.

여 저는 정말 재미있는 직업을 갖고 있답니다. 여러분이 돈을 좋아하신다면 제 일을 정말 좋아하실 거예요. 사람들이 하루 종일 저에게 와서 재정적인 문제로 상담을 합니다. 저는 그들이 계좌에 입금하고 출금하는 것을 돕습니다. 가끔 저는 사람들에게 차를 사거나, 집을 사거나, 아니면 심지어 사업을 시작하도록 대출을 해줍니다. 저는 제가 지역사회의 중요한 일부라는 느낌이 들어서 제 일을 사랑합니다.

10

M Do you have any ideas about your future career?

W I'm not sure. I'm thinking of being a teacher.

M That's a great career. What do you want to teach?

W History, mostly. It's the subject that most interests me. What about you?

M I'm planning to go into politics.

W In what way?

M I think it would be fun to work on political campaigns.

남 진로에 대해서 생각하는 게 있어?

여 확실하지는 않아. 선생님이 될까 하고 생각 중이야.

남 그거 좋은 직업이다. 뭘 가르치고 싶은데?

여 주로 역사. 내가 제일 재미있어하는 과목이거든. 너는 어때?

남 난 정치계에 입문하려고 해.

여 어떤 식으로?

남 난 정치 운동을 하는 것이 재미있을 것 같아.

11

[The telephone rings.]

M Hi, this is George Smith from Room 204.

W Hello, Mr. Smith. How can I help you?

M I'm having a problem, actually. The air conditioner isn't working.

W I'm very sorry to hear that. I can send a repairman by the end of the day.

M But it's very hot today. I don't think I can wait that long.

W I'm sorry, sir. It's the best I can do.

M Well, I don't think this is very good customer service.

[전화벨 소리]

남 안녕하세요. 저는 204호의 George Smith입니다.

여 안녕하세요. Smith 씨. 무엇을 도와드릴까요?

남 사실 문제가 있어요. 에어컨이 작동하지 않아요.

여 정말 죄송합니다. 수리하시는 분을 오늘 저녁 때 보내드리겠습니다.

남 하지만 오늘 무척 덥잖아요. 그렇게 오래 기다릴 수 없을 것 같은데요.

여 죄송합니다. 그게 제가 할 수 있는 최선입니다.

남 음. 고객 서비스가 그렇게 좋지는 않군요.

12

W What did you think of the concert last night?

M I found it really exciting. The band put on a great performance.

W I agree. I love how they smashed their guitars at the end.

M I know! That was so cool.

W We have to see them again when they come back to our city.

M Without a doubt! It's a date, then.

여 어젯밤 공연 어땠어?

남 아주 신났어. 밴드가 훌륭한 공연을 했어.

여 나도 그렇게 생각해. 난 그들이 마지막에 기타를 부순 게 좋았어.

남 알아! 정말 멋졌지.

여 그들이 우리 도시에 다시 올 때 꼭 다시 보러 가야 해.

남 당연하지! 그럼 약속이다.

13

① W Thanks for helping me with my math work.

   M No problem. I'm glad you understand it now.

② W Would you like to study together?

   M I'd love to, but I have other plans.

③ W Are you going to science class?

   M Yes, I'm on my way there now.

④ W What's the problem, Daniel?

   M I can't find my calculator anywhere.

⑤ W Excuse me, do you know the way to the bookstore ?

   M I'm sorry, but no. I'm new here.

① 여 수학 숙제 도와줘서 고마워.

   남 뭘. 네가 이제 이해하니 다행이다.

② 여 같이 공부할래?

   남 그러고 싶은데 다른 계획이 있어.

③ 여 과학 수업에 가는 거야?

   남 응. 지금 가는 길이야.

④ 여 왜 그러니. Daniel?

   남 어디에서도 내 계산기를 찾을 수가 없네.

⑤ 여 실례합니다. 서점으로 가는 길을 아세요?

   남 죄송합니다만 몰라요. 여기 처음 와서요.

14

W   Dear Diary: My day started out pretty badly. It was raining this morning. I got all wet and messed up my hair. Then I forgot my homework and got a bad grade in class. On top of that, I was given a whole pile of homework to do. So I was feeling pretty down. But then something cool happened. James asked me out on a date for the weekend. I'd been waiting for him to ask, and I was so happy he did. It made my whole day better.

여   오늘의 일기: 오늘은 아주 안 좋게 시작했다. 아침에 비가 오고 있었다. 나는 온통 젖었고 머리가 엉망이 되었다. 그 다음에 나는 숙제를 잊어버려서 수업에서 나쁜 점수를 받았다. 거기다가 엄청나게 많은 숙제를 받았다. 그래서 나는 기분이 아주 좋지 않았다. 그런데 그때 뭔가 멋진 일이 생겼다. James가 나에게 주말 데이트 신청을 한 것이다. 나는 그가 나에게 물어보기를 기다리고 있었고, 실제로 그래서 너무 기뻤다. 그 일은 내 하루 전체를 더 좋게 해주었다.

15

M   Hi. I'm here to pick up my dog.

W   Of course. Let me get your bill.

M   Thanks.

W   All right. We did some tests. Those cost $30.

M   OK. What else?

W   We gave her some medicine for worms. That's another $15.

M   That sounds reasonable. Anything else?

W   Just the bath. That's $10.

M   Great. So what's the total bill?

남   안녕하세요. 강아지를 찾으러 왔습니다.

여   네. 계산서를 가져다 드리겠습니다.

남   감사합니다.

여   좋습니다. 우리는 검사를 좀 했어요. 그게 30달러입니다.

남   네. 또 다른 건요?

여   벌레 때문에 약을 좀 주었어요. 그게 또 15달러이고요.

남   괜찮은 가격 같네요. 다른 것은 없나요?

여   그냥 목욕이요. 그건 10달러입니다.

남   좋습니다. 그래서 총 가격은 얼마죠?

16

M   I can't wait for the music festival this weekend.

W   I know. Three whole days of great bands and fun times.

M   Did you buy our tickets yet?

W   No. I think we have to buy them at the gate.

M   Oh no! Look at this. They were only sold in advance. And now they're sold out!

W   I'm so sorry! I didn't know. I should've asked.

M   Listen, it's disappointing, but we can always go next year.

남   이번 주말에 하는 음악 축제가 너무 기다려져.

여   알아. 멋진 밴드들과 즐거운 시간을 보내는 3일이 되겠지.

남   표는 샀어?

여   아니. 입구에서 사야 하는 것 같아.

남   오 이런! 이걸 봐. 표는 미리 파는 것밖에 없었어. 그리고 지금은 매진이야!

여   너무 미안해! 몰랐어. 물어봤어야 하는데.

남   내 말 들어봐. 실망스럽긴 하지만 언제든 다음 해에 갈 수 있잖아.

17

M Congratulations on winning the tennis match!

W Thanks so much, Stephen. I'm really happy about it.

M That other player never had a chance. I've never seen you play so well.

W I was really in the zone, I guess.

M What do you mean by that?

W Oh, it's an expression. It means I was very focused.

M I see. Anyway, I think you're good enough to play professionally.

남 테니스 경기에서 이긴 것 축하해!

여 정말 고마워. Stephen. 나 정말 기뻐.

남 상대방 선수가 기회를 한 번도 얻지 못했어. 네가 그렇게 잘 하는 걸 본 적이 없어.

여 정말 집중했던 것 같아.

남 무슨 뜻이야?

여 아. 그건 표현이야. 내가 정신을 아주 잘 모았다는 뜻이야.

남 알겠다. 어쨌든 넌 프로로 경기를 해도 좋을 정도로 잘 하는 것 같아.

18

M Everyone needs something to do in their spare time. For years now, I've had the same hobby. It's fun because I get to be creative with my designs. I like to use lots of colors. Also, it's great to make things, and watch them come together. But it's also practical. While I'm enjoying my hobby, I'm also making something useful. For instance, I gave my cousin a scarf for Christmas last year.

남 누구나 여가 시간에 할 일이 필요하다. 이제 몇 년이 되어가는데. 나는 똑같은 취미를 가져 왔다. 디자인으로 창의성을 발휘할 수 있어서 재미있다. 나는 많은 색을 사용하는 것을 좋아한다. 또한 조각들을 만들고 그것들이 합쳐지는 걸 보는 것은 즐겁다. 하지만 그것은 실용적이기도 하다. 나는 취미를 즐기면서 또한 무엇인가 실용적인 것을 만든다. 예를 들어 나는 작년 크리스마스에 사촌에게 스카프를 주었다.

19

① W What do you think of my new glasses?

   M They make you look so smart!

② W Excuse me. What's the next stop?

   M I think it's the Market Street station.

③ W What's the problem, Gene? You look mad.

   M I'm just frustrated with the heavy traffic today.

④ W Have you seen my blue shirt anywhere?

   M No, I like the red one better.

⑤ W Can I get you anything else to eat, sir?

   M No, thank you. I'll have the check now, please.

① 여 내 새 안경 어떻게 생각해?

   남 그거 쓰니까 너 정말 똑똑해 보여!

② 여 실례합니다. 다음 역이 어디인가요?

   남 Market Street 역인 것 같아요.

③ 여 왜 그래. Gene? 화가 나 보여.

   남 그냥 오늘 차가 너무 막혀서 짜증이 났어.

④ 여 혹시 내 파란 셔츠 어디서 봤어?

   남 아니. 난 빨간 게 더 좋아.

⑤ 여 드실 것을 더 가져다 드릴까요. 손님?

   남 아니에요. 됐습니다. 이제 계산서를 가져다 주세요.

20

M Hey, Marla. Can I get a ride home?

W Sure, hop in. I'll be happy to take you home. But first, you must put your seatbelt on.

M Really? I never wear a seatbelt in my car.

W Why not? They're for your safety!

M I know, but they're so uncomfortable.

W Would you rather be injured in a wreck?

M You've got a good point. I'll put it on.

남 야. Marla. 나 좀 집에 태워다 줄 수 있어?

여 그럼. 타. 기꺼이 데려다 줄게. 그런데 먼저 안전벨트를 해야 해.

남 정말? 난 내 차에서 안전벨트를 절대 안 하는데.

여 왜 안 해? 네 안전을 위한 건데!

남 알아. 하지만 너무 불편해서.

여 차 사고 나서 다치고 싶니?

남 네 말이 맞다. 벨트 할게.

모의고사 3회

| 01 ② | 02 ③ | 03 ③ | 04 ② | 05 ① | 06 ① | 07 ② | 08 ① | 09 ⑤ | 10 ④ |
| 11 ③ | 12 ⑤ | 13 ⑤ | 14 ② | 15 ⑤ | 16 ④ | 17 ④ | 18 ② | 19 ③ | 20 ② |

01

W What's the best way to get to the library from here, Mac? I'm in a hurry.

M Well, that depends. You could always get a taxi.

W Too expensive for me. Does the bus go by the library?

M Yes, that would be the fastest way.

W What about the subway? Wouldn't that be faster?

M Not really. You'll have to walk several blocks.

W OK. Well, I'm in a hurry, and I don't have much money, so I guess the bus is best.

여 여기서 도서관으로 가는 가장 좋은 방법이 뭐야. Mac? 나 시간이 없어.

남 음. 경우에 따라 다른데. 언제든 택시를 탈 수 있지.

여 나한테는 너무 비싸. 버스가 도서관을 지나가니?

남 응. 그게 제일 빠른 방법일 거야.

여 지하철은 어때? 그게 더 빠르지 않을까?

남 별로. 몇 구역을 걸어야 할 거야.

여 알겠어. 음. 난 시간이 없고 돈이 별로 없으니까 버스가 제일 낫겠다.

02

W In today's news, a hurricane is expected to hit the coast of Florida within the next 24 hours. The storm will be quite severe by the time it reaches the coast. Experts expect there to be a great deal of damage from

여 오늘의 소식입니다. 앞으로 24시간 내에 허리케인이 플로리다 연안을 강타할 것으로 예상됩니다. 폭풍이 해안에 닿을 때쯤이면 매우 심해질 것입니다. 전문가들은 바람과 홍수로 인해 상당한 피해가 있을 것으로 예상하고 있습니다. 주민들은 그 지역에서 대피하고 가능하면 다른 곳으로 대피하

wind and floods. Residents have been asked to leave the area and seek shelter somewhere else if they can. We'll have more on this as the story develops.

라는 당부를 받았습니다. 진행 상황이 입수되는 대로 전해드리겠습니다.

03

M ① A woman is buying shoes.
② A man is shopping with his wife.
③ The woman is selling the man shoes.
④ The man is showing off his new shoes.
⑤ The woman thinks the shoes are ugly.

남 ① 여자가 신발을 사고 있다.
② 남자가 부인과 쇼핑을 하고 있다.
③ 여자가 남자에게 신발을 팔고 있다.
④ 남자가 새로 산 신발을 자랑하고 있다.
⑤ 여자는 신발이 흉하다고 생각한다.

04

M Did you see the soccer match last night?
W Yes, it was very exciting.
M It's the first time we've beaten Brazil.
W I know. One of our best players got an injury, though.
M Yeah, but he'll be fine. I can't wait for the finals next week.
W It's going to be a great game. I hope we win!

남 어젯밤에 축구 경기 봤어?
여 응. 정말 재미있었지.
남 우리가 브라질을 꺾은 건 처음이야.
여 알아. 그렇지만 제일 잘 하는 선수 중 한 명이 부상을 당했어.
남 그러게. 하지만 괜찮을 거야. 다음 주 결승전이 너무 기다려져.
여 굉장한 경기가 될 거야. 우리가 이기면 좋겠다!

05

W Dear Mr. Park,

My name is Gail, and I'm a parent of one of your students. I just want to write to you to express my appreciation for all your good work this year. My son has made better marks this year than any other, and I think it's all because of you. He says you are a wonderful teacher, and I agree.

Sincerely, Gail Forest

여 친애하는 Park 선생님께

제 이름은 Gail이고 선생님의 학생 중 한 명의 부모입니다. 올 한 해 동안 선생님의 노고에 대한 감사를 표하고자 편지를 씁니다. 올해 제 아들은 다른 어떤 해보다 좋은 성적을 받았고, 저는 그것이 모두 선생님 덕분이라고 생각합니다. 그 애는 선생님이 훌륭한 선생님이라고 말하고, 저도 동감입니다.

Gail Forest 드림

06

W Hi, Mike. Would you like to study after school?
M That sounds great. I could use some help in math.
W How about 5:00?
M I have basketball practice until 5:00. Can you give me an hour to rest and change?

여 안녕. Mike. 학교 끝나고 공부할래?
남 그거 좋지. 수학에 도움을 좀 받을 수 있겠다.
여 5시 어때?
남 난 5시까지 농구 연습이 있어. 쉬고 옷 갈아입을 시간을 한 시간 줄 수 있니?

W That might be too late for me, actually. How about three hours before that?

M You mean before practice starts? Sure.

W Great. I'll see you later.

여 사실. 그럼 나한텐 너무 늦을지 몰라. 그것보다 세 시간 전은 어떠니?

남 연습 시작하기 전에 말이야? 좋지.

여 좋아. 이따 보자.

07

M I bought this lamp yesterday, but when I opened the box, it was broken.

W Oh, I'm very sorry, sir. Would you like to exchange it for another?

M No, thank you. I don't think I want this type of lamp if it breaks so easily.

W Well, we have a large selection of other lamps, if you'd like to buy another.

M Thanks, I'll do that. Can I get my refund for the broken lamp now?

W We don't do refunds, but I can give you store credit.

남 이 램프를 어제 샀는데 상자를 열었을 때 깨져 있었습니다.

여 오. 정말 죄송합니다. 손님. 다른 제품으로 교환하시겠습니까?

남 아니요. 됐습니다. 이렇게 쉽게 깨지는 종류의 램프는 안 되겠어요.

여 저. 다른 제품을 사기 원하시면 저희 가게에 다른 램프도 종류가 많이 있습니다.

남 감사합니다. 그렇게 할게요. 이 깨진 램프에 대한 금액을 지금 돌려받을 수 있을까요?

여 저희는 환불은 해드리지 않지만 가게 적립금을 드릴 수 있습니다.

08

M I think it's time for me to buy a new car.

W Really? What type of car are you looking for?

M Well, I want to be friendly to the environment.

W So I guess that means no big truck, right?

M No, I don't want a truck. Maybe a small car.

W That's a great idea. They don't use much fuel, and they cost less, too.

M Or I could buy a scooter. Lots of people ride them these days.

W Scooters can be kind of dangerous in heavy traffic though. I don't want you to get hurt.

남 나 이제 새 차를 사야 할 때인 것 같아.

여 정말? 어떤 종류의 차를 찾고 있어?

남 음. 난 환경 친화적이면 좋겠어.

여 그러면 커다란 트럭은 안 되겠다. 그렇지?

남 안 돼. 트럭은 별로야. 아마 작은 차가 좋겠지.

여 그거 참 좋은 생각이다. 작은 차는 연료가 많이 들지 않고 값도 싸지.

남 아니면 스쿠터를 살 수도 있겠어. 요즘 많은 사람들이 그걸 타더라.

여 하지만 스쿠터는 교통량이 많을 때 좀 위험할 수 있어. 난 네가 다치는 걸 원하지 않아.

09

M What a game this is, folks! If you're just joining us, the Tigers and Giants tied the game in the second inning with one point each. The Giants pulled ahead in the third inning with one more run, but the Tigers

남 굉장한 경기입니다. 여러분! 지금 막 시청하신 분들을 위해 말씀드리자면, 2회에 Tigers와 Giants가 1점씩 따서 동점을 이루었습니다. Giants는 3회에 1점을 더 따서 앞서 나갔지만 Tigers가 반격해서 4회에 2점을 추가해 리드를 잡았습니다. 각 팀은 5회에 1점씩을 추가했고요.

came back and took the lead in the fourth inning with two runs. Each team scored one run in the fifth inning, and the Tigers scored a run in the top of the seventh.

Tigers가 7회 초에 1점을 추가했습니다.

10

M What did you think of the movie, Kate?

W It was fun. But it wasn't my favorite.

M Why do you say that? I thought it was great!

W It was exciting, yes. But for a horror movie, it wasn't very scary.

M Oh, I see what you mean. I guess I didn't mind that, since there was so much action.

W Maybe next time we can see a scarier movie.

남 영화 어땠어. Kate?

여 재미있었어. 하지만 내가 제일 좋아하는 종류는 아니었어.

남 왜 그렇게 말해? 난 정말 좋았는데!

여 흥미진진하기는 했어. 하지만 공포 영화로서는 별로 무섭지 않았어.

남 아. 무슨 말인지 알겠다. 나는 액션이 많아서 그건 별로 신경 쓰지 않았던 것 같아.

여 다음 번에는 더 무서운 영화를 보자.

11

M I've done these math problems over and over, but I never get the right answer.

W Do you mind if I take a look at it?

M Sure. You're better at this than I am.

W Hmm, All of your numbers are correct. But I think the method you used is wrong.

M What would you suggest?

W Let's try this. Use this other method to solve the problem instead.

M Oh, that makes sense. Thanks!

남 이 수학 문제들을 풀고 또 풀어봤는데 맞는 답이 안 나오네.

여 내가 한번 봐도 될까?

남 그럼. 넌 나보다 수학 잘 하잖아.

여 흠. 네 숫자들은 모두 정확해. 하지만 네가 사용한 방법이 잘못된 것 같아.

남 어떻게 하면 좋을까?

여 이렇게 해보자. 대신 이 다른 방법을 써서 문제를 풀어보는 거야.

남 어. 그거 말 되네. 고마워!

12

W Hi, Charles. Did you get my message about the meeting?

M No, did you try to call me?

W Yes, it was last night. I left a message on your phone.

M Oh, I see. My phone has been erasing messages lately. I think it needs repairs, but I don't have a lot of money.

W Why not just get a new one? It's probably cheaper.

M I'll think about that. Thanks, Pam.

여 안녕하세요. Charles. 회의에 대한 제 메시지 받으셨어요?

남 아뇨. 저랑 통화하려고 하셨어요?

여 네. 어젯밤에요. 전화기에 메시지를 남겼어요.

남 오. 알겠어요. 제 전화기가 최근에 메시지를 지우고 있어요. 수리를 받아야 할 것 같은데 돈이 별로 없어서.

여 그냥 새것을 사시지 그래요? 그게 아마 더 쌀 거예요.

남 그걸 생각해 봐야겠네요. 고마워요. Pam.

13

M Do you like a good scare? Do you want to be truly terrified this Halloween? Then come down to the House of Screams—the best haunted house in town! We'll be open from five o'clock to one o'clock on October 31st. Admission is $5, but groups of four or more get a discount! And if you're brave enough to show up at midnight, we'll take 50% off the price of admission!

남 깜짝 놀라는 걸 좋아하세요? 이번 할로윈에 정말로 놀라고 싶으세요? 그렇다면 마을 최고의 유령의 집인 '비명의 집'으로 오세요. 우리는 10월 31일 5시부터 1시까지 열려 있을 것입니다. 입장료는 5달러이지만 4인 이상의 단체는 할인을 받습니다! 그리고 자정에 나타날 정도로 용감하시다면 입장료에서 50%를 할인해 드리겠습니다!

14

M We have reviewed your application, and we are very pleased. We are happy to say that you are accepted to City High School. Congratulations! Included you will find reading materials about our school. Also, there is a schedule of events for the new student orientation in the Spring. You will register for your new classes then. In the meantime, you will be contacted by the school to arrange for the payment of tuition.

남 우리는 당신의 지원서를 검토했고 아주 흡족합니다. 우리는 당신이 시립 고등학교에 합격되었다는 것을 말씀드리게 되어 기쁩니다. 축하합니다! 우리 학교에 대한 안내 책자를 첨부합니다. 그리고 봄에 있을 신입생 오리엔테이션 행사 일정표도 있습니다. 그때 새로운 수업에 등록하게 됩니다. 그러는 동안 등록금 지불 방법을 의논하기 위해 학교로부터 연락을 받게 될 것입니다.

15

W Hi, Mr. Adams. Your car is ready for you.

M Thanks. How much do I owe you?

W Well, the wash was $6.

M OK. And the new tires?

W You got two of them, at $50 each?

M That sounds right.

W Lastly, we changed the oil, which was $20.

M OK. Just give me the total and I'll pay now.

여 안녕하세요. Adams 씨. 당신 차가 준비되었어요.

남 고맙습니다. 얼마 드리면 되죠?

여 음. 세차비는 6달러였어요.

남 네. 새 타이어는요?

여 각각 50달러에 두 개 하셨죠?

남 맞는 것 같아요.

여 마지막으로 저희가 오일을 갈아드렸는데 그게 20달러였습니다.

남 알겠습니다. 총 금액을 알려주시면 지금 지불할게요.

16

W Would you like to have lunch tomorrow?

M I'd love to, but I can't. I'll be at the park.

W Oh, what are you doing at the park?

M I'm volunteering for a city program, picking up litter.

W What do you mean?

M Oh, trash that people throw on the ground.

여 내일 점심 먹을래?

남 그러고 싶은데 안 되겠어. 공원에 있을 거야.

여 오, 공원에서 뭘 하는데?

남 시 프로그램에 자원봉사를 신청했어. 쓰레기 줍는 일이야.

여 그게 무슨 뜻이야?

남 오, 사람들이 땅에 버리는 쓰레기 말이야.

W I see. Well, that's very kind of you.

M We could always use more volunteers. Do you think you'd like to help?

W Sure. I'll see you tomorrow.

여 알겠어. 음. 그거 참 착한 일인데.

남 자원봉사자는 언제나 더 받을 수 있어. 너도 돕고 싶니?

여 그럼. 내일 보자.

17

W The Greeks are a very important people in history. They loved to study the arts, like poetry, theater, and even science. Many of our ideas today come from Greek scientists long, long ago. And we still read plays and poems written by the Greeks. The best example is *The Odyssey*, written by Homer thousands of years ago. Many school children still read this great poem.

여 그리스인들은 역사에서 아주 중요한 사람들입니다. 그들은 시. 연극 같은 예술과 심지어 과학도 즐겨 연구했습니다. 오늘날 우리가 갖고 있는 개념 중 많은 것이 아주 오래 전 그리스 과학자들로부터 온 것입니다. 그리고 우리는 아직도 그리스인들에 의해 쓰여진 희곡과 시를 읽습니다. 가장 좋은 예가 호메로스가 수천 년 전에 쓴 「오딧세이」입니다. 많은 학교의 학생들이 아직도 이 위대한 시를 읽습니다.

18

M Excuse me. Can you direct me to the bank, please?

W Of course. From the hospital, go straight on Third Street.

M OK. What then?

W Pass one street and take a left at the next one.

M Oh, that's near the school. OK, and then?

W Take the first right. The bank will be the first building on the left.

M Thanks so much for your help!

남 실례합니다. 은행으로 가는 길을 가르쳐 주시겠어요?

여 그럼요. 병원에서 Third Street로 쭉 가세요.

남 알겠습니다. 그 다음에는요?

여 거리를 하나 지나고 다음 거리에서 왼쪽으로 꺾으세요.

남 오. 그러면 학교 근처네요. 알겠어요. 다음에는요?

여 처음 나오는 오른쪽 길로 꺾으세요. 은행은 왼쪽에 있는 첫 번째 건물일 거예요.

남 도와주셔서 정말 감사합니다!

19

W Are you ready for the track and field competition?

M Yes, I've been training very hard. Especially for the long jump event.

W What else are you competing in?

M Um, the 100-meter race for sure, and the high jump.

W Cool. Are you not running the relay race this year?

M No, I didn't like it last year. Besides, I think I have enough to do.

W Well, best of luck to you!

여 육상 대회에 나갈 준비 됐니?

남 응. 난 무척 열심히 훈련해 왔어. 특히 멀리뛰기 시합을 위해서.

여 다른 경기에는 어떤 것에 참가하니?

남 음. 100미터 경주는 당연히 나가고, 높이뛰기도 해.

여 멋지다. 올해는 계주 달리기는 안 뛰니?

남 안 나가. 작년에 별로였거든. 게다가 충분히 할 게 많아서.

여 그래. 행운을 빈다!

20

M Can you believe this traffic? It's crazy!

W It's a crowded city, Jim. What do you expect?

M I don't even know why I bother driving.

W Don't worry. Everyone else is frustrated too.

M You don't seem to be frustrated.

W It doesn't bother me. With so many cars on the road, it makes sense that there are traffic jams.

M Yeah, well, it's making me crazy.

W Maybe if you just relaxed, it wouldn't be so bad.

남 차가 이렇게 많은 게 믿어져? 정말 심하다!

여 복잡한 도시잖아. Jim. 뭘 기대했니?

남 내가 왜 굳이 운전을 하는지조차 모르겠네.

여 걱정 마. 다른 사람들도 모두 짜증날 거야.

남 넌 별로 짜증난 것 같지 않은데.

여 난 짜증 안 나. 차에 차가 이렇게 많으니 차가 막히는 게 당연하잖아.

남 그래. 음. 난 너무 화가 나.

여 좀 마음을 편히 가지면 그렇게 나쁘지 않을 거야.

센치한 Listening 길들이기

중학 영어 내신 만점을 향한 길들이기 시리즈

- 센치한 Listening 길들이기 총 6권
- 도도한 Reading 길들이기 총 6권
- 까칠한 Grammar 길들이기 총 6권

(주)컴퍼스미디어